Jerusalem Calls

This work is dedicated with love and a tender heart to the memory of Sam and Olive Cornwell, who folded me into their hearts and their lives in those very first days. Their adoption of me as their "spiritual daughter" has been one of the great treasures and privileges of my life. The world's loss of these two—during the writing of this book—is heaven's great gain.

Contents

Foreword

Once I read the first chapter of this book, I could not put it down. I had never seen the world through the eyes of a young woman who grew up in a Jewish family. Through her story, I was reminded that none of us choose our family of origin or their religious beliefs, yet we are deeply influenced by our childhood experiences.

It was captivating to see the author embrace the religion of her family and to develop a deep reverence for God and His relationship with her ancient ancestors. Even more amazing was to observe that same God reach out to her during her college years and open her eyes to Jesus, who was also born into a Jewish family. As she embraced the Messiah, the rituals of her childhood took on even deeper meaning.

In this book, Tammy Priest walks through the pilgrimage feasts of ancient Israel. She shares not only what God was teaching the Israelites and what it looked like for their descendants to celebrate in Jerusalem but also what Christians today can learn of God's love, faithfulness, protection, and guidance.

I predict that as you read this book, you will read the Old Testament with a much deeper appreciation of God's love for us revealed in Jesus. Each of the pilgrimage feasts reminds us of different aspects of God's character. The God of ancient Israel is the same God who revealed Himself by sending His Son to open the door to Jews and gentiles to a personal relationship with Himself. This book has the potential of enriching your own relationship with God.

Gary Chapman, PhD
author of The 5 Love Languages
and God Speaks Your Love Language

CHAPTER 1

Jerusalem Calling

> Jerusalem built up, a city knit together, to which tribes would make pilgrimage, the tribes of the LORD . . . as was enjoined upon Israel—to praise the name of the LORD.
>
> Psalm 122:3–4 JPS

I turned thirteen on Friday the thirteenth.

Sounds spectacularly unlucky, I know. It was, in fact, the exact opposite. On that sweltering day during the summer of 1982, I found myself in the company of eleven other awkward thirteen-year-olds and their parents—or, in my case, grandparents. We were a band of Jewish pilgrims in the middle of Jerusalem, just like our ancestors all those years ago.

Well, not *just* like them. We had flown from JFK in a jumbo jet instead of caravanning across the desert on beasts of burden. And we passed the time sipping on chilled Coca-Colas and reclining in cushioned seats. So not *just* like them. But we twelve children of Abraham, Isaac, and Jacob were there, in the city that God had chosen for His name to dwell, that ancient place of pilgrimage—and there's no place I would have rather been (Deut. 16:11; Ezra 6:12).

Israel's collision of antiquity and modernity entranced me from the instant I stepped out of the airport and into the living diorama of stone, sand, and desert blooms. I remember the bus ride to Jerusalem creating the sensation of time travel as our jetlagged eyes brimmed with wonder. We gazed and gaped as landmarks of legend greeted us. Road signs casually pointed the way to ancient places like Jericho and Bethlehem right alongside mileage markers to gas stations and shopping centers. As we drew closer to Jerusalem's hill, the marvel of it all engulfed me. Scripture was coming to life before my eyes. Ancestors were coming to life before my eyes. Layer upon layer of biblical narratives stacked up along the roadside, surrounding us like a great cloud of witnesses, encouraging us as we embarked on this literal journey of faith.

Almost three thousand years ago, psalmists described Jerusalem as the joy of the whole earth and the perfection of beauty (Pss. 48:2; 50:2). But their words of adulation hadn't remotely prepared me for what I would encounter there. They hadn't prepared my heart and mind and soul for what I would discover about the Land, about my people, and about myself. Without warning, every olive tree, artifact, and arid breeze began to draw me in like an unrelenting force. For every night of that two-week pilgrimage, as my head sank heavily into crisp hotel pillows, I felt more and more like I had finally made my way home.

I realize that probably sounds melodramatic. But the truth is that much of my life to that point had already seemed like a never-ending series of pilgrimage journeys—only those regular pilgrimages always left me feeling like I was never *quite* home. These journeys began when I was three years old, after my parents divorced and my mom and I moved from outside Washington, DC, to the Midwest. Soon I began traveling back and forth on my own, under the watchful care of flight attendants, from one blended family to the other. I jetted across the country three times each year, like the ancient pilgrims traveled three times each year to their Father's house in their nation's capital—only my journeys were not a worship experience. Instead of anchoring me like the ancient pilgrimage did for the Israelites, my journeys left me feeling unmoored most of the time. Belonging here and belonging there, I didn't feel like I fully belonged anywhere.

Except, that is, in Brooklyn. My grandparents' cozy, brick duplex is where I came home as a newborn, just after my father frantically arrived from basic training to meet his first child. It was there that I learned to say "bird" in my grandma's arms and watched nature unfold in her little garden. Brooklyn is where I witnessed my grandparents' abiding love and where I learned about God's. It was where I first began to love the Lord my God with all my heart and mind and soul and strength. And so it was there that He first began revealing Himself to me. He revealed Himself through each flickering flame and every chanted prayer. Through each morsel of broken matzah and every sip of sweet wine. I was drawn by the language of holiness and redemption whispered through fire and food. And joy. So much joy.

Whether spoken through a prayer at dinner, a verse on the wall, or a lesson about loving my neighbors, it seemed that Adonai was always present on East 29th Street. He spoke light from the menorah on the shelf and sustenance from the challah on the table. He whispered faithfulness through the tiny brass figures of Hannah and Samuel (my grandparents' biblical namesakes). He received worship through the silver-plated, turquoise-studded prayer book that rested in the dining room. And He revealed His steadfastness through the countless heirlooms and tchotchkes that lined their shelves and hung on their walls. Every square inch of their home was filled with quiet testimonies of God's love.

And now, my grandparents had brought me, their eldest grandchild, to Jerusalem to celebrate my entrance into Jewish adulthood: becoming a bat mitzvah, a daughter of the covenant. Despite the violence simmering at the Lebanese border, our eyes were set on Jerusalem. We would be in God's hands, in God's land, for this rite of passage. And I had been preparing for months for the group ceremony, learning my portion of the prayers and Scripture. I wish I could put my hands on those assignments now, to reflect on them with older and wiser eyes and with deeper and richer faith. But those papers have been lost to multiple years, multiple households, and multiple lifetimes, it seems. Whatever those prayers and verses were, I was ready to chant them with our little congregation of pilgrims in the synagogue ruins on top of Herod's mountain: Masada.

Of course, I would also have a stateside ceremony in the fall. My entire extended family—and a handful of my non-Jewish junior high friends—would pack our modest little synagogue in Ames, Iowa.* Small and utilitarian as the building was, our house of worship—built on the edge of an Iowa cornfield just three years earlier—was a treasure. No more renting rooms or bowling alleys or spaces in churches, which is how the congregation gathered and worshiped for its first seventeen years of existence.[1] The Ames Jewish Congregation would now welcome my large Northeastern family to the rich black soil of the heartland.

My October ceremony would be the very first bar or bat mitzvah on record in our college town, and I had put in a year of diligent study and preparation under the guidance of our part-time, commuting rabbi. I would wear a smart, purple velvet suit delivered from Manhattan for the momentous occasion. My loved ones and school friends would hear me chant the ancient prayers. They would listen to me read the first chapter

*I was the only Jewish kid in the whole middle school.

of Genesis in Hebrew, from a Torah scroll that had been rescued from Prague during World War II. And then they would receive my homily on the passage.

We would all celebrate together that night wearing our prettiest party dresses, our sharpest suits, and our broadest smiles. We would fill the Memorial Union at Iowa State University with singing and dancing and feasting and laughter. And my toddler sister would cap off the evening with her unforgettable belly dance in the middle of the ballroom's parquet floor—a moment that still maintains its place in family lore.

But there was none of that at the top of Masada. No big crowd. No live band. No belly dance. And I didn't long for one ounce of it on that scorching, summer morning. Instead, I relished the profound simplicity of establishing my personal covenant with God in the barren beauty of Israel. I wore a simple white cotton top, embroidered with just a handful of bright flowers around the neckline. And, together with my fellow pilgrims, I entered Jewish adulthood within the ruins of the oldest synagogue ever discovered outside of Jerusalem.[2] That day—and all the days and moments enveloping it—established itself as an anchor to who I was and would become.

Not that I suddenly understood everything there was to know about God in that mountaintop moment. I still don't, of course. Who of us does? But what astonished me was the profound weight of God's holy places and the way they grounded me. They grounded me not with the weight of ancient stones or weathered bronze but with the weight of impossible promises both made and kept, and through ancestral roots that pushed down deep through blowing sand into immovable bedrock. Those roots reached back not only a few generations or centuries but millennia, carved into the landscape of earth and history.

I couldn't articulate all that philosophizing in that moment. I certainly couldn't articulate it on that Friday the thirteenth, the day before our ceremony. My only concern on that very lucky summer day was getting the Hebrew right when my turn came to chant from the Torah scroll. That was, after all, the whole reason we were there. Not for the camel rides or the Dead Sea swim. Not for our recognition at the Knesset or our visit to Galilee. Not even to stand on the Mount of Olives or pray at the Western Wall. We had come to worship and to lead worship, to become sons and daughters of the covenant, and to become adults in the eyes of our community and in the eyes of God. And so, as the sun went down on my thirteenth birthday, we all honored the Sabbath together, sharing the sacred cup and bread and candlelight, beckoning God to prepare us for the day ahead.

The next morning—groggy with fatigue and jittery with nerves—we arrived at the base of the mountain before daybreak and began the steep ascent to the ancient fortress of Herod the Great. Or what was left of it, at least. After Herod died in 4 BC, Rome took possession of the opulent compound.[3] Although Jewish resisters managed to retake the fortress in AD 66, they were no match for the eight thousand Roman troops who breached the walls six years later.[4] The nearly one thousand Jewish zealots, priests, and refugees could do nothing but watch as the soldiers constructed a ramp up the sheer cliffside.[5] Stories of those Jews' bravery always intrigued me growing up. According to Josephus, they resisted Rome even in death, taking one another's lives through an intricate, methodical plan. It was a defiant refusal to be taken captive yet again in their own land, this time by Titus, the Roman officer and later emperor who had just burned Jerusalem to the ground.

Now, almost two thousand years later, I was making footprints in the same rocky sand and gazing on the same beautifully desolate view as those brave ancestors. I would pray the even more ancient prayers and read from the even more ancient Scriptures—the same prayers and Scriptures that those ancestors had also held dear. And I would do so within the ruins of their synagogue. It was astounding, and my heart still swells when I think about it.

For all that momentousness, though, the service itself was a quiet affair. It was sacred yet beautifully informal. We sat shoulder to shoulder on the tiered, first-century benches. Herod's broken stone walls surrounded us, and the clearest blue sky stretched over us. Touristy sun hats covered our heads, and xeroxed programs fluttered in our hands. Then the rabbi called our Hebrew names one by one. At each of our turns, we rose to stand with him, accompanied by our father, or—in my case—grandfather. My grandma captured a photo of Grandpa, the rabbi, and me standing together in that moment, our three heads bent over the text. Her view of us that morning sits on my desk today, encased in acrylic. When the sun shines through it, the scene lights us up just like it did on that glorious August morning.

I remember reading from the Torah, confident and nervous all at once. I was reading the Scriptures just a few feet from where archaeologists had unearthed ancient scrolls of Deuteronomy and Ezekiel.[6] I stood only steps from where a cache engraved with "Priestly Tithe" had been excavated.[7] I was a modern girl reading from the ancient Torah, and I was overwhelmed with the understanding that I was part of something—and *becoming* part of something—beyond my comprehension. All of us were. We closed the service with the beautifully minor-key *Oseh Shalom* prayer, asking the One who causes peace to reign in the heavens to let that peace descend on us as well.

Joyful shouts of *mazel tov!* rose and mingled together as hugs and handshakes passed all around.* And then I froze, eyes wide with incredulity, transfixed by a box filled with Torah scrolls. It had been tucked safely to the side, out of the way of our dusty

*"Mazel tov" literally means "good fortune" and is said as an expression of congratulations or blessing over a special event or happy news.

feet and water canteens. Each scroll was majestically "dressed" (the traditional term) in navy velvet. Loops and braids of golden trim adorned the edges. Embroidered tablets of the covenant celebrated the treasure inside. And peeking through the top of each luxurious mantel were twin wooden finials, securing the Scriptures rolled up inside.

Each magnificent scroll bore the name of a newly minted child of the covenant embroidered in thick gold letters—including mine. I was now officially a daughter of the covenant, being gifted my very own scroll of the covenant. The photograph Grandma snapped of the twelve of us gazing down at the treasure in our hands is one of my favorites from the whole trip. You can almost see the stress and jitters of the morning melting into deep pools of gratitude and wonder.

Soon, though, the early rising and soaring temperatures caught up with us teenagers and elders alike. Wilted from the blistering heat and drained by the occasion, we allowed the gondolas to carry us down from our mountaintop experience. Our whole company trudged across the broiling parking lot, filed quietly onto the bus, and collapsed onto the sticky vinyl seats. For the next hour, we all mused privately through dusty windows. The Dead Sea sparkled on one side and the Judean hills radiated from the other. It seemed that the Promised Land was celebrating us, embracing us, and lulling us into shalom. Even as my eyelids drooped, that velvet treasure remained clutched in my arms.

Later that evening, refreshed by naps and showers, our little congregation bid adieu to the Sabbath during a celebratory banquet. The hotel ballroom startled in its contrast to the morning's setting, greeting us with the clinking of crystal, the blaring of music, and the presentation of a sheet cake so big that it boasted each one of our names in black icing, written in both English *and* Hebrew. A giant *mazel tov* was piped in the corner.

Grandma proudly salvaged my personalized sliver of frosting, presenting the prize to me on a royal blue napkin: *Deborah bat Michael*. Deborah (my given Hebrew name, after my great-grandmother), daughter of Michael. Ever the pack rat, I strategized throughout dinner about how to bring home my little bit of buttercream, intact on the blue damask, from Jerusalem to JFK to DC to Iowa. Unfortunately—or fortunately, for our luggage—a photo would have to suffice. That picture has survived four decades, definitely a longer shelf life than buttercream circa 1982.

It didn't really matter, though. My name stitched in gold was a much sweeter treat than the one piped with sugar. Forty years later, that Torah scroll remains one of my most prized possessions. Holding it still ignites a wave of warmth in my chest, transporting me back to the Land. It pulls me back to that ancient synagogue, where I first stepped into my place as a daughter of God's covenant, to that day I became *Deborah bat Michael, bat mitzvah*. Touching the soft velvet connects my heart to the Land where I sensed I was truly home, to the place promised to my ancestors. To Abraham, Isaac, and Jacob, and to Sarah, Rebecca, Rachel, and Leah.

With each day of our trip that summer, I understood more profoundly that I was not a tourist. I was a partaker. A partaker of the Land and of the promises. I could see them, touch them, and smell them. I touched the limestone of Solomon's Wall and wept with my grandmother at Rachel's tomb. I gathered shards of First Temple pottery from an excavation taking place right under a family friend's Jerusalem home. I looked out their kitchen window to trace the road our Messiah was promised to walk when He arrived to set all things right one day.

During those extraordinary days, I began to comprehend both the vastness and the intimacy of God's promises for the very first time. It was a weight that anchored and freed me all at once. I *belonged*. To this place, to my people, and to the God who spoke it all into being. I was home in a way I hadn't been before. I was beginning to find rest for my soul.

When the day of departure finally arrived, I hated leaving. I remember being gripped by an inexplicable ache as I gazed through the airplane window, watching the Land grow smaller and smaller, losing its detail in our swift ascent. During those fourteen days of my thirteenth year, I had become completely, irreversibly tethered to the Promised Land. Woven into her, and Zion woven into me. I *needed* to come back. And to *keep* coming back.

Maybe that's exactly how God wanted the Israelites to feel about Jerusalem. Maybe He wanted them to yearn for that place of wonder and worship, where His glory mysteriously dwelled. Maybe, by reuniting in Jerusalem three times each year and celebrating amid the throngs of far-flung friends and family, God's children would find their hearts and minds and souls and strength anchored. Anchored to the point that, whenever they were absent from Jerusalem, living in the distant places they officially called home, each person would sense that a foundational piece of themselves was missing. They would always feel that they were never quite settled and never quite home. Never, that is, except when they returned to the one place God had chosen as a "dwelling for his Name" (Deut. 12:11 NIV).

> Three times a year—on the Feast of Unleavened Bread, on the Feast of Weeks, and on the Feast of Booths—all your males shall appear before the LORD your God in the place that He will choose.*
>
> (Deut. 16:16 JPS)

Looking back on that pilgrimage command, it seems so straightforward to us today. It probably sounded straightforward to the pilgrims in Jesus's day, too. But for the people who

*Despite the phrase "all your males" in this verse, other verses in the chapter specifically refer to men, women, and children coming to worship before the LORD for the feasts, as does the Talmud.

first received it in the wilderness of Sinai, God's command wasn't straightforward at all. They had to read between all the lines. And when they did, God dared them to believe more than they had ever allowed themselves to think or imagine.

You see, when God first uttered that pilgrimage command, His people were still just a band of newly freed slaves wandering around in the wilderness. They hadn't even built the tabernacle yet. And once they did, they would have to carry that magnificent house of worship through the desert for another thirty-nine years, picking up stakes every time God called them to move. It was a herculean task, and God's priestly tribe became expert movers, as well as ministers, in the wilderness. Teams of Levites labored to roll up the four layers of roofing that protected the tabernacle from sun, rain, and wildlife—and from the eyes of the people. They did the same for the walls and for every bit of rope that held it all together.

Arms that normally carried wicks and spices switched gears to carry crossbeams and frames, stacking the gilded lumber across a doublewide caravan of wagons.[8] Hands that usually played instruments stopped to pack silver sockets and rings and stakes. God's ministers loaded the laver and the lampstand, the tables of Shewbread and incense, and the altar. The *altar*. I wonder what must have gone through the Levites' minds every time they hoisted that massive bronze structure, stained with the blood and ashes of so many sacrifices.

How unbelievably *heavy* the tabernacle must have been. Not only the structure, but the weight of the glory it contained: the ark of the covenant. Wherever they went, the people carried with them that most sacred center of the sanctuary, the earthly resting place for God's glory. That golden box with its cherubim wings on top and the second set of tablets inside must have been a constant reminder—even cloaked beneath the veil and badger skins and blue cloth—of both their desperate failure and God's abounding mercy (see Num. 4:5–6).

Because, despite the golden calf debacle, which left the first set of tablets in pieces at Moses's feet, God had not left them. Instead, He leaned in. And this reality must have made the people's rare glimpses of the cloaked ark a beautifully reassuring sermon in itself. Especially considering the name God had given for the ark's lid: the mercy seat. Even in the middle of the wilderness, God was demonstrating that His heart is bent toward mercy and grace.

The mercy seat's occupant vacated His earthly throne every time Israel packed up to move through the desert. I simply cannot begin to imagine what it was like to witness God's Shekinah sweep out from the Holy of Holies into that soaring pillar above all their two million heads, or to look on as the priests took hold of the golden poles and hoisted God's throne onto their shoulders (Exod. 12:37).* And then, weary from bearing the burden of such majesty under the searing sun through the shifting sand, watch them set up the whole tabernacle once again. I wonder if they ever got used to the otherworldliness of it all. I hope not.

Just as difficult for me to comprehend about this process—this dismantling and transporting and rebuilding of the holy places and holy things—is the way we read about it so matter-of-factly today. With such nonchalance and detachment. *The veil, the ark, the cloud, blah, blah, blah* . . . How can we do this? How can *I* do this? Moses's description of heaven's fire and cloud should take our breath away *every single time*. Maybe it's that we've become too familiar with the Exodus account from years of Sunday school felt boards or have grown unimpressed with the supernatural after a steady diet of apocalyptic, CGI superhero movies.

**Shekinah* is from the Hebrew word for "dwelling" or "settling" and is used in both Jewish and Christian theology to refer to the glory of God's presence (Kaufmann Kohler and Ludwig Blau, "Shekinah," in *The Jewish Encyclopedia* [Funk & Wagnalls, 1906], 258).

But whether we minimize it or romanticize it, carrying the tabernacle through the desert was, quite literally, a beautiful burden. The Israelites knew the full weight of God's presence in a way the rest of us never will. It must have been so very much to carry in their hands, their hearts, and their heads. It must have been utterly exhilarating, but also utterly exhausting. It was a regular reminder for God's people that, even though they were finally free, they didn't have a home, a place where they belonged.

Today, we have the luxuriously deceptive gift of hindsight and written Scriptures. Of course they are going to get to the Promised Land! Of course they will stop setting up a temporary worship center in the sand and have their very own building of limestone and marble and gold! Of course they will be spread throughout all of Canaan and need to take vacation time to go worship in God's presence! But for the ones who had walked through the Red Sea to freedom, the wilderness was all they knew and all they had.

And so, when I read God's pilgrimage command in the Torah, I don't see a command at all. Instead, I see an incredibly tender promise. I see a staggering pledge that one day, these weary refugees would have their very own nation. I see an assurance that, one day, their descendants would worship at a permanent sanctuary instead of a portable tent. God's people would no longer be nomads, and God's glory would no longer dwell in a tent. One day, journeying would become a joyful time of grand reunions and sacred worship. Through His words of pilgrimage, God was breathing life and hope into Israel's weary souls.

But why three pilgrimages each year? Isn't that excessive and expensive, given how long the journeys and feasts lasted? And why gather for those particular feasts? Why not for all of them, or for just one? Why not the Day of Atonement, the holiest day of the whole year, when they would all be made right with God? Why did God choose to call everyone in ancient Israel out of their personal spaces and places to worship with one another in Jerusalem for the Feast of Passover, the Feast of Weeks, and the Feast of Booths?

To be perfectly honest, I never really thought about it growing up. With the ancient Temple and its sacrificial altar buried beneath two thousand years of stone and strife, there is nowhere to pilgrimage anymore. At least not for the prescribed worship. So instead, we fifteen million Jews now scattered around the globe celebrate in our own homes and local synagogues. And it is wonderful. For my entire childhood, I marveled that Jewish people all around the world were chanting the exact same prayers and performing the exact same rituals on the exact same days as me. We may not have been reuniting face-to-face in Jerusalem, but we were all woven together in worship, synchronized across multiple continents and cultures.

Years later, as I grew into my faith, I would begin noticing things about these three feasts that I had never known to look for during that first pilgrimage to the Promised Land. In 1982, though, I only knew what I knew. And so, just like my ancestors had wistfully returned to their hometowns after their Jerusalem pilgrimages, I wistfully returned to mine. But also just like them, Jerusalem had whispered my name, beckoning me to return. I heard it. I felt it. That first pilgrimage awakened in me a longing and tug for *home*. It's a tug that isn't really about a place at all, but about presence: *His* presence. It's about who I am when I am within it, and who we are when we stand within it together.

Jerusalem calls.

CHAPTER 2

Making Way

I rejoiced when they said to me, "We are going to the House of the Lord."

Psalm 122:1 JPS85

I couldn't stop thinking about the contraband hidden inside my suitcase. I was convinced that security would find it wrapped up in my white cardigan, wedged down deep in the back corner of the suitcase under my tennis shoes. Oblivious to my panic, a multigenerational sea of Orthodox men in their long black coats and tall black hats seemed to spill into every spare inch around my family in the El Al waiting area as we waited for our plane. Each man was reverently wrapping his arm and forehead with tefillin, bowing at the waist, and chanting the ancient prayers.* They all appeared to be lost in

*Tefillin is a set of two small, black leather boxes containing four passages of Scripture. They are worn around one's arm and on the forehead, held in place with attached straps (wrapped around the arm seven times, and once around the head to fit snugly). The four passages are Exodus 13:1–10; Exodus 13:11–16; Deuteronomy 6:4–9; and Deuteronomy 11:13–21, all of which speak to God's command to bind His instructions "as a sign upon your hand and between your eyes."

their own worlds of worship, even in the midst of that very public place.

I took in the scene with a mixture of admiration and trepidation, certain they could see right through me—and into my suitcase. But the men kept right on praying, unaware of my smuggling and my paranoia, and undistracted by the din and grime and sauna that was the JFK airport that summer day in 1990. The truth is, I knew they wouldn't stop to watch the commotion even if I was exposed. But my grandmother would. I feared she would be leading the charge. And that thought gripped my heart with panic and grief.

A quick glance at my Swatch watch reminded me that it had been exactly one week—almost to the hour—since I had met Jesus in a little church in rural Virginia. I hadn't wanted to be there that day. I *hated* being there, in fact. But there I had been, just seven days before departing on my second journey to Israel. A single moment inside that white cinderblock sanctuary turned my entire life upside down. God's audible voice had flooded my ears, wrecking and redeeming everything I thought I understood about Him. And now just a week later—with my heart a mess of emotion—I was setting off with my father's side of the family to the Holy Land. It was our once-in-a-lifetime family pilgrimage. The thirteen of us would celebrate my grandparents' anniversary together in the Land they loved.

Sitting there at JFK, surrounded by the Orthodox men and my non-Orthodox family, I was still trying to wrap my brain around the impossibly bizarre reality that I—*Deborah bat Michael*—was now bootlegging a tiny New Testament under the nose of my grandma and grandpa, my father and stepmom, my aunt and uncle, and my sisters and cousins. *What was I thinking*? This could get a lot messier than the buttercream I had wanted to smuggle in my bag eight years earlier. Had it really been that long since I had taken hold of the beautiful Torah scroll at the top of Masada? Had it really been eight years since I felt Jerusalem's call and her anchoring tug? It seemed like barely a day, yet also an eternity.

Returning from that first pilgrimage during my thirteenth summer, my heart remained tethered to Jerusalem. I embraced my heritage, cherishing it just like my grandparents had always hoped. Soon after our return, I had my big stateside bat mitzvah ceremony in Iowa. My mom and stepdad crafted a celebration that was beautiful, festive, and warm.* Everyone on every side of my extended, blended family danced and sang and laughed together. My friends and I sang on the stage with the band. We all ate fruit from a watermelon basket that featured my name carved into the rind. It may not have been embroidered velvet like my Masada scroll, but it was sweet and special and filled me with joy. The whole weekend brimmed over with loved ones and love. I had completed a *second* bat mitzvah ceremony, this time in a modern sanctuary filled with well-versed family and uncertain friends. I found myself standing a little straighter, a little taller.

Unlike so many Jewish kids my age, instead of checking out after my bat mitzvah, I dove in. I started teaching Hebrew school to the young children at our synagogue. In high school, I asked permission to create a synagogue youth group, even though there were only four of us at the time. I was beginning to understand that a faith community of peers was important—*especially* because there were only four of us. So I launched our group and led it until I graduated. And secretly dated a Jewish college boy in our congregation for good measure. (Sorry, Mom.)

Setting off on my own college adventure that fall, my father made an unannounced stop on the way to the dorms. Parking outside the Hillel house, we left the old Volvo station

*My mom and stepdad married when I was five years old. So while I refer to him as "stepdad" here for the purpose of clarity, I've called him "dad" ever since that day, at my request. I was fortunate to grow up with two dads who love me very much, and I them.

wagon—stuffed to the gills with my clothes and Matisse posters and suitcase-sized Brother word processor—in the care of my stepmom and little sisters. A few minutes later, I emerged with a lifetime membership to the international Jewish organization for college students. I spent a good bit of time around Hillel during my years at the University of Virginia. By the end of my third year, I became the board liaison between Hillel and the Jewish Student Association (JSA). JSA was purely social, mind you—lots of nice Jewish guys meeting nice Jewish girls. And my role as liaison actually captured my identity pretty well at that point. I was a Jewish girl who loved her heritage but who also wanted to go out and have fun.

That's not to say that I spent my time exclusively with other Jewish students. Not by a long shot. Between my involvement in sorority life and student union leadership, the majority of my friends (and boyfriends) were not Jewish—not unlike my whole Midwestern upbringing. You would think, then, that I knew a thing or two about Christianity. But I did not. I knew absolutely *nothing* about what Christians believed.

Most of my childhood friends were churchgoers. Some of my college friends were, too. But most of them attended Sunday morning services after a Saturday night of partying. Their everyday lives and habits didn't seem any different from mine, so nothing ever led me to wonder about their faith. Plus, in all those years, no one ever talked about Jesus. No one talked with me about who Jesus was, what He did, or why. Not once, ever. Not even when I went to a friend's church lock-in during junior high. There was just lots of music and food and playing tag in the sanctuary. To the pastor's credit, when I politely declined Communion in the morning due to my being Jewish, he immediately exclaimed, "We love you, too!"

It's not entirely true, though, that *no one* shared Jesus with me. A few people did share over the years. As in, "You need Jesus, or you're going to go to hell!" These exhortations always came from people who didn't know me—like the guy who sometimes handed out pocket Bibles near Cabell Hall. Those champions of the gospel never actually took time to explain who this Jesus was or why He died on a cross. They never talked with me about His love and grace. I only heard about my singular flaw: my Jewishness. And so, to my ears, the message was that I was a problem to be fixed; a project, not a person. I never heard that Jesus *shared* my heritage. I never heard that His Jewishness was the foundation of His identity as Savior. I never heard that my very own Scriptures foretold Him, that they had *promised* Him. So I simply assumed that Christians believed in some other god, which I knew was wrong. That was in the Ten Commandments, after all. I did feel a bit sorry for them for believing such a strange, sad story, though.

While I may have been indifferent toward my friends' nominal religion, I hated the Christian church as an institution. I had grown up learning about the Spanish Inquisition and Russian pogroms, about forced conversions and the Holocaust. I had read Hitler's quotes about Jews and learned that European churches hung swastikas from flagpoles during World War II. The Holocaust, I therefore surmised, was about Christians hating and killing Jews.

Anti-Semitism impacted my own circles, too. Grandma Arliene especially loved to tell me about her cousin Philip, who was rejected by New York University's medical school in the 1930s, to the dismay of his college advisor. Suspecting anti-Semitism, the advisor took it upon himself to resubmit Philip's application, replacing his Jewish-sounding last name with something more generic. Philip was promptly accepted, and all the cousins chipped in to pay his way.* In my own modern life, my throat tightens when I hear people tell jokes about Jewish

*Philip's branch of the family tree now bears the name his advisor used on that second application.

people or when I see anti-Semitic comments from celebrities. Fear strikes me when I see swastikas at protests and violence at synagogues. I've never understood how Americans could fight passionately against Hitler yet deny my people access to schools and jobs and organizations here in the United States. At the end of the day, I grew up thinking that religious Christians were misguided and a little strange at best. At worst, I thought, they were fanatical and genocidal. So I became defensive and hostile toward anyone who broached "Jesus talk" with me.

Until, that is, the summer of my second pilgrimage.

It was supposed to be my last summer as a carefree college student. Instead, I was participating in a mandatory student leadership program at school. Adding insult to injury, I had to live in a dorm with a bunch of students I didn't know—student government types, or "politicos," as we called them. I wasn't a politico. I was one of the three student union chairs, and my particular job was to plan parties—large-scale, university-wide parties, but parties nonetheless. University Union's student reach was significant, and we were considered student body leaders along with our elected politico peers. The administration's goal was for us to spend the summer building collaboration across our organizations. This included housing us together in unairconditioned dorm rooms and making us play softball every week. Seriously. We didn't get our (very small) paycheck if we didn't play.

In any event, one of those politicos, T. J., invited me to an InterVarsity gathering. "A *what*?" I asked. He clarified: InterVarsity Christian Fellowship. Music, hanging out, and a little "talk." The miracle of his invitation is not that I said yes, because I didn't. Having nominally Christian friends was one thing, but attending a Christian event was quite another. No, the miracle is that I didn't shun him like the plague. Maybe that's because my refusal simply elicited a shrug and an "Okay," as if I had simply turned down a late-night run to McDonald's. There was no judging, shunning, or warnings of brimstone.

Despite his low-key reaction, however, I soon discovered that T. J. was one of those born-again Christians. I realized this not because of anything I heard him say, but because other students made fun of him behind his back. *Jesus freak. God squad.* You've heard the labels. Maybe you've used them. I certainly did. But because he never pushed anything religious after that InterVarsity invitation, I decided to overlook this rumored character flaw. Soon, T. J. was one of five people I became especially close with that summer. That crew already knew one another from their student government roles, and it seemed that they, too, had chosen to ignore his flaw.

Except I shouldn't really call those five a "crew." Because I quickly gathered that they didn't really spend time together as a group outside of our summer program. They navigated different social circles, came from different backgrounds, and practiced different politics. I honestly couldn't see a single thing that united them. Yet they *were* united. And they welcomed me into their fold. It was the first time I had been part of genuine friendship among people who held such wildly different views and lifestyles. There was some sort of camaraderie among them that I hadn't figured out. Whatever it was, I found myself drawn in.

Halfway through the summer, the parents of another student invited our whole leadership group to their home in Richmond for the weekend. It was, in fact, the weekend before the day in question at JFK airport. These kind parents thought we could use some TLC and a few home-cooked meals. Bless them. About fifteen of us took them up on their offer, including two of my new summer friends—Donna and the "Jesus freak." The three of us hopped into my old Chrysler LeBaron convertible and headed east on Interstate 64. Our hosts greeted us with a delicious meal and air-conditioning.

In the middle of laughing and unwinding late into Saturday night, my road trip companions pulled me aside to ask about plans for the morning. *You mean where to watch the men's*

Wimbledon finals? Nope. That's not what they meant. They wanted to get up early and go to church. Still misunderstanding their intent, I began mentally calculating the risk of my father's ire if I were to let them borrow my car. But I needn't have worried—at least not about that—because these wonderful new friends weren't asking for my keys. They wanted me to take them. To go with them. To church. *Ummm, no,* said my raised eyebrow and silent stare. I had never gone to church except for a few weddings, and there was no way I was going to start just because of some sleepover.

But I had a problem. Several problems, actually. The church where Donna and T. J. wanted to worship was in Palmyra, a tiny town almost all the way back to Charlottesville. This meant we would need to stop there on our way back to school. I wanted to suggest they find another ride, maybe from someone who had an actual interest in church—or, who at least wasn't *opposed* to it. But the whole reason they wanted to go to this tiny church in rural Virginia was that another friend from our summer leadership program was its part-time pastor.

Wait, I thought. Trevon was an ordained *minister*? As a *college* student? Are you *kidding* me? I was both impressed and panicking. I had spent the entire summer telling my leadership peers they needed to appreciate the experience of Jewish students at UVA. I had talked about the need to consider our unique circumstances as well as the prejudices and exclusions we faced. Now I was being asked to attend an African American church with two of my new friends, where another of our friends served as the pastor. If I refused, I knew I would look like a complete hypocrite. I could lose all credibility among my peers and our faculty advisors. Yet I was mortified at the thought of setting foot inside a Christian worship service. My brain played out the entire dilemma in a split second. I realized that I couldn't say no. And the realization made me angry.

Early the next morning, I found myself stepping carefully over all the sleeping bodies that carpeted the den floor, quietly muttering to myself. In contrast to our boisterous drive to Richmond the day before, we three now spent the entire drive to Palmyra in silence. My born-again passenger rode shotgun, speaking up only to tell me when it was time to turn here or there. My displeasure was palpable, I'm sure. We arrived late, only adding to my aggravation. I dreaded the prospect of drawing unwanted attention. *Look at the Jewish girl walking into our Jesus-freak gathering*!

Stepping through the doors, though, my nerves eased ever so slightly as I caught sight of UVA students filling half the pews. Which, to be honest, didn't take much. The Haden Chapel sanctuary is only twenty feet across—I've looked it up. But the sight of those fellow students meant that we weren't the only ones who had come to support Trevon. I exhaled, feeling the tiniest bit of relief. Maybe my classmates would simply take note of my presence as proof that I was a supportive (which I was) and openminded (which I was not) friend.

Scanning the sanctuary, I noticed my friend Jenny sitting by herself. I made a beeline toward her, wordlessly leaving the other two behind in the wake of my discontent. I remember walking down the aisle, my heart pounding violently. The sound filled my ears like something out of "The Tell-Tale Heart." Silently I prayed, begging God to please forgive me for being in a church. *Please*.

Startled by my unexpected presence next to her, Jenny looked up and smiled widely in surprise. She handed me her hymnal, already opened to the page where they had begun singing. Again, I prayed. I promised Adonai that if the song had *that name* in it, I wouldn't sing. But if the words were simply "God" or "Lord," I would sing to *Him*. Everyone else could sing to whoever they wanted. That was on them, not me. I don't remember the name of that hymn, but I do remember that, written in small italics underneath the title, there was a short verse from the Psalms. I quickly skimmed the lyrics and, indeed, there was no mention of *that* name. So I softly began to sing.

I had only managed to get out a few words when a voice interrupted me. I wish I could describe it. All I can say is that it was loud and soft and strong and gentle, all at once. And this is what the voice said—out loud—to me: "Jesus is the Son of God. He is the Messiah." I stood, frozen. Everyone else continued to sing, oblivious to the voice. Could no one else hear it? Hear *Him*? In those moments, everything slowed. Sound. Thoughts. Breath. Time.

I turned slowly to Jenny, wide-eyed—maybe wild-eyed. She shot me a quick, reassuring smile and kept singing. Jenny probably figured that her Jewish friend was feeling understandably uncomfortable. But uncomfortable is not how I felt. *Stunned* is how I felt. I was stunned by the voice that filled my ears and by the message that it spoke. *That is who Jesus is?* I had never, ever heard this before. Not in my whole entire life. Yet in that moment, instead of skepticism, I felt shockingly anchored, just as I had on top of Masada eight years before. Because, even though I had never heard that voice before, I knew exactly Who it belonged to. And He was making all things new.

I remember stepping outside after the service into the midday sun, dazed by the light flooding my eyes and the voice still echoing in my head. I locked eyes with T. J. and paused. "I need to talk to you when we get back," I said. I *had* to confide in someone. And I figured that—based on T. J.'s rumored and ridiculed zeal for Jesus—he was the one person who wouldn't think I was completely out of my mind. The three of us buckled up and headed back to Charlottesville in silence, just like our trip to Palmyra had been. But this time, I was silenced by awe instead of anger.

Back at the dorm, after dropping my bag inside my door, I climbed the stairs apprehensively to T. J.'s suite. I hoped I hadn't misjudged his faith or overestimated his belief. Would even *he* think what I had experienced was impossible? But it wasn't doubt that washed over his face as I told him about the voice; it looked like a mix of thrill and wonder. It turned out that T. J. had been praying for me all summer. And so had his friends and family back home. Had God really answered all their prayers so dramatically? Had God moved through the audacious prayers of my other four friends and their people back home, too? Because, of course, that was the invisible glue I hadn't comprehended before: their common faith in Jesus as Messiah. They had all been praying that God would lead and that God would speak. They just hadn't expected Him to answer with audible words.

The way God moved that morning in Trevon's church impacted each of us, my friends and me. Not only that summer but through the years to come. Over time, so many memories from my pre-Palmyra life began to surface. I began to see that conversations, situations, and decisions over the course of my first twenty-one years had dotted my path all the way to that moment in Haden Chapel. I recognize them as graces radiating through space and time. Seemingly disconnected points and people that God had been weaving together, drawing me toward that day, that pew, and that presence.

When I reflect on all the graces that had ushered me toward Palmyra, my thoughts often gravitate to the pilgrimage roads that led to ancient Jerusalem. I marvel at the abundance of people and effort preparing the way for my ancestors to reach the Temple. Every spring, workers set about fixing and smoothing and straightening the roads washed out by winter's rain. Others scooped the gloppy mess out of countless wells through the countryside so that pilgrims could find refreshment along the way. Teams crushed lime and mixed it with water, whitewashing tombs to warn weary travelers away from uncleanness.[9] Sentinels formed outposts for pilgrims coming from as far as Babylon, protecting them through the desert's dangers.[10] And every Jewish household in the land donated a half shekel to pay for it all.[11] The whole effort strikes me as a beautiful snapshot of all of God's people helping all of God's people answer Jerusalem's call.

More kindnesses awaited the pilgrims once they reached Jerusalem. Cobblers worked during non-assembly days to repair shoes tattered from the journey.[12] Priests invited visitors into the courtyard to see the Shewbread, which—even though the loaves had been removed from the Holy Place after the previous Sabbath—was now miraculously radiating heat.[13] This was said to be evidence of God's favor upon their pilgrimage. So many locals provided lodging at no cost to the visitors, because Jerusalem was considered to be home for them all.*

Sometimes I try to visualize this entire pilgrimage process playing out from a bird's-eye view. I imagine it would be a thrill to watch a time-lapse video: so many people trickling from all directions, joining together to form streams, the streams merging to create rivers, and the rivers finally spilling into a sea of humanity around the Temple. What a wonder it would be to see upwards of three million pilgrims amassing at God's holy hill.[14] I wish the Israelites who first received the pilgrimage command could see this view from above, too. Surely they would marvel at the sight of their descendants traveling toward the gleaming Temple from so many directions and distances. Maybe they would take it all in with wonder and song, like they did on freedom's side of the Red Sea. Their hearts would swell to behold their children's children worshiping at that magnificent dwelling place of God, living in the fulfillment of His bold promises made in the desert wilderness.

*Upon leaving Jerusalem, pilgrims typically gifted their hosts with the hide(s) of their sacrifices and their empty wine jug (B. Avot D'Rabbi Natan 35:2; B. Yoma 12a:6; Deutsch, Eisenstein, and Franco, "Pilgrimage," in *The Jewish Encyclopedia* [Funk & Wagnalls, 1906], 36).

I wish we could watch all the pre-pilgrimage preparation, too—to see everything being readied before the travelers even hit the road. It would be inspiring and humbling to observe all those weeks of arduous effort that made the whole pilgrimage possible in the first place, undertaken by people the pilgrims didn't know and probably never saw. We would witness the very real and practical reality that—whether the journey was a half-day walk from Bethlehem or a three-week trek from Babylon—all of God's people needed help making their way to Him. Just like I needed help on *my* road to that monumental moment in Trevon's church. People had loved me well. They loved me with their friendship and prayers, with their words and their kindnesses.

Including that little New Testament I tucked into my suitcase just a week after Palmyra. Every night of our family pilgrimage, I quietly unearthed T. J.'s borrowed Bible from its hiding place and tiptoed through the darkness to the hotel bathroom, stepping over my family's clutter of shoes and backpacks. There I would sit, cross-legged on the cold tile, soaking up John's Gospel by the light of a little flashlight as I read it for the very first time. I remember the apostle's words bringing the word to life, each verse putting flesh on this Messiah that the voice had revealed to me. I may have accepted Him in Palmyra's miraculous moment, but now I was beginning to know Him.

In the stillness of those nights, huddled by myself in the dark, I first came to see Jesus. And in the light of each new morning, I walked in His steps. I took in the very places where Jesus lived and breathed, died and rose. They were the same places I had walked eight years earlier, but now I saw them with fresh eyes and a new heart. The timing of that second pilgrimage was such an incredible gift, such a lavish kindness of God. And, once again, I hated to leave.

I'm sure my ancestors were sad to leave Jerusalem, too. But they knew they would be back in just a few months for the next feast. And even their departure was a celebration. They offered up a blessing over all the priests and Levites who had ministered to them, singing most appropriately from the concluding song of the pilgrimage psalter:[15] "Look! Praise the LORD, all you servants of the LORD, Who stand by night in the LORD's house! Lift up your hands in the sanctuary. Praise the LORD!" (Ps. 134:1–2 HNV). In response, the priests chanted the third and final verse over their departing brethren: "May ADONAI, the maker of heaven and earth, bless you from Tziyon" (Ps. 134:3 CJB). Just as the priests had welcomed the joyful pilgrims into Jerusalem with Aaron's blessing, they now sent them home with David's benediction.*

But there was none of that for me when I left the Promised Land on that sweltering summer day. There was no blessing, no song. And all I felt was an ache. It was the same ache that had taken me by surprise eight years earlier. That tug—now pulling even stronger—told me that home, in its truest sense, was once again the place I was leaving. Home was still Jerusalem. Yet now it was a place I had never imagined before. I was leaving a Jerusalem that held an empty grave, a Jerusalem that I could actually carry with me and within me.

As our plane ascended and the Land disappeared, I felt that my anchor was giving way. Not in the sense of breaking loose or becoming unmoored. Instead, I felt the anchor plunging deeper, attaching me to the very foundation beneath all the magnificent layers of shadows and symbols and rituals and promises. It was pulling me into the presence of the Ancient One Himself, a place where my pilgrimaging ancestors never imagined they could step. Deep calling to deep.

Jerusalem still calls.

*Although Psalm 134 does not provide authorship within the psalm, most commentators agree that David is the likely author.

CHAPTER 3

Pilgrimage Soundtrack

Your priests are clothed in triumph; Your loyal ones sing for joy.

Psalm 132:9 JPS85

Mr. Flugel-Flaggle visited the Brooklyn brownstone quite often when I was young.

I mean, I knew it was Grandpa. But his complete sincerity and quirky accent drew me in, even when I was old enough to resist. We grandchildren drank in his stories with rapt delight. Invariably though—usually at the most crucial moment in his tale—Mr. Flugel-Flaggle's strength would vanish, drained suddenly and completely by his excited storytelling. His head would loll and his eyelids droop. And—though I always chose to ignore it—the tiniest of smiles would curl at the corner of his mouth. He didn't have to suppress the smile for long, though, because Grandma's singsong alert would ring out just as quickly from the next room. "Oh, dear! Mr. Flugel-Flaggle needs *energy*!" And that was our cue. Like the release of so many tightly wound springs, we would all leap onto his lap with a barrage of hugs, kisses, and laughter. It was our valiant and always successful effort to revive our favorite, silly guest.

If memory serves me correctly, Mr. Flugel-Flaggle even earned a mention at Grandpa's funeral. Everyone, adults and children alike, loved my grandpa's alter ego. Looking back now, I think what I treasured most about Mr. Flugel-Flaggle is that, even though my grandfather spent his days addressing complex problems with his engineering brain, he was forever showing us the importance of playfulness, creativity, and laughter. Even at eighty years old, he ignored my grandma's panicked protests and got down on hands and knees in the middle of my living room floor to give his three-year-old great-grandson horsey rides on his back.

As much as I loved Mr. Flugel-Flaggle's visits and his fantastic stories, I adored the real man even more. No matter the setting or subject, Grandpa's soft voice commanded attention—not through force or fear, but through its scarcity. His wife was the talker. Grandma's lilt, laughter, and strong opinions filled every room she entered. Grandpa, on the other hand, offered up words like rare gems. He would watch and listen, watch and listen, then watch and listen some more, to the point where I sometimes wondered if he had drifted off or tuned us out. But then his quietly confident voice would wash over the room, thoughtfully knitting everything together with an assessment that left us looking like a collection of bobblehead dolls, all nodding at his wisdom. Except for Grandma, whose mind was almost always already made up. She would smile and wave him off with an "Oh, Sam!" Those two were opposites of the most magnetic kind, and had been ever since they met in junior high.

Just days after their wedding—still teenagers—Grandpa had headed back to his Army Air Corps base for training. As a World War II bombardier, he lost most of the hearing in his left ear during a harrowing mission. But, unlike many people with hearing loss, Grandpa's voice didn't loudly overcompensate.

He was all about content over volume and substance over flash. Which meant that everyone—family, friends, coworkers—leaned in to listen, seeking him out in all sorts of predicaments. Whether it was something as serious as handling an asbestos exposure in a city building or something as small as helping his granddaughter choose an Italian-ice flavor, Grandpa's words held incredible weight. Which is why I missed them so deeply during the rift following my road-to-Palmyra experience.

I didn't blame him, though. I didn't blame *any* of my family. I knew I had lobbed a smoke bomb into the middle of everything, making it difficult for us to make our way toward one another. During those days, my heart was a swirling stew of emotions—joy and wonder mixed with guilt and grief. At one point the friction and my guilt swelled to the point that I withdrew from potentially painful interactions, which, as you can imagine, only served to deepen both the friction and my guilt. Brokenness often begets brokenness, it seems. Yet also simmering in that emotional stew were memories that I savored. So many family memories sustained me until God, in time, stitched us all back together. Those sustaining memories included my grandpa's words of love, wisdom, and laughter from my prior twenty-one years.

One of those childhood talks still replays in my mind. It was a quiet afternoon, and Grandpa was sitting in the dusty-blue, velvet wingback chair. He patted his knee, ushering me to one of my very favorite perches. I could tell, though, that this wasn't a rescue mission for an energy-depleted Mr. Flugel-Flaggle. No, this was Grandpa, and his tone was serious. It was the same voice I sometimes overheard when he took a call from the mayor's office or spoke with the rabbi on a Saturday morning. "I'm going to tell you something very important," he said. My eyes grew wide. In that magical childhood moment, Grandpa confided that, because of our family lineage, I was, in fact, a princess. A *princess*! Shrieking on the inside, I composed myself as every good princess should. But honestly, I was pretty distracted. I felt like I had stepped into a fantastical fairy tale, the ones where an average girl discovers that she is truly royalty.

Except that I'm not. I had completely misunderstood. And I didn't stand corrected for years, during which time my daydreams grew and blossomed under my very attentive care. A few years later, when I was finally unable to contain all the dreams and questions I had cultivated, I approached Grandpa to learn more about our lofty pedigree. And, with all the seriousness and humility of a princess prepared to accept her mantle, I asked him to tell me more about our relatives. "You know, the ones who make us royalty. Who make me a princess."

His brow furrowed for a moment. And then, instead of nodding proudly, my grandfather let out a laugh. His still-bright blue eyes twinkled and his still-dark red hair swayed as he shook his head, chuckling. Seeing the crestfallen face of his eldest grandchild, he quickly composed himself. "No, *bubala*." Grandpa smiled gently.* "Not 'princess.' *Priestess*. You're a priestess. We are Levites. Our family is from Aaron." In that singular moment, I felt all my elementary-school daydreams shattering, tiny shards falling in slow motion into the shag carpet at our feet. Masking my devastation as best I could, I weakly returned Grandpa's smile.

"That's . . . *incredible*." I forced the word, as if Grandpa's correction had given way to a greater treasure, as if it were the most incredible news I had ever received in my entire life. But it was not. Not at that moment, at least. Still, I sat and listened, nodding to the voice I loved, hearing my grandpa share about the heritage he loved. I wish I had realized on that day how amazing this revelation truly was. I wish my disappointment had given way to genuine joy in a matter of seconds instead of years. And

*"Bubala" is a Yiddish term of endearment, usually for a child, similar to "sweetheart" or "sweetie."

I desperately wish that his 400-year genealogy record hadn't disappeared during their later move to Syracuse.

Over time, though, I slowly unwrapped the gift of my grandfather's words. And as I did, so many other things began to make sense, like why he usually stopped at the synagogue on his way to work in Manhattan. I think Grandma is the one who told me that Grandpa took this regular detour to make sure there was a *minyan*—the quorum necessary to hold an official prayer service. I realize now that he probably took that on with the heart of a priest, making sure people were able to draw near to God in community. And I understood why, during my father's childhood, my grandfather would be called to the front of the sanctuary on Shabbat. There, he and the other *kohanes*, or "priests," would lay prostrate before the Lord as the rabbi unrolled the Torah scroll. Maybe Grandpa always seemed to measure his words with extra care and kindness because he was the priest in the room.

I wish I had asked him a hundred more questions about what being a *kohane* meant to him. When I was finally ready to dig deeper into our heritage and history, dementia was beginning to steal all his answers. Even so, I can still hear Grandpa's voice. His words about our family still echo in my thoughts, and I wouldn't trade them for anything—not even for a princess's crown. After all, royalty can be deposed and overthrown, but ancestral roots are immovable, plumbing deep through millennia of relationships and history and faith. All those roots had begun to anchor me even before I understood them, calling to me, drawing me closer.

On this side of Masada's ceremony and Palmyra's voice, the knowledge that I'm a Levite—a *priestess*—still makes my heart swell with wonder.** I, *Devorah bat Michael*, am in the family

**I also love imagining the twinkle in God's eye when, after marrying my husband, David, my last name became "Priest."

of Miriam the prophetess, that brave sister of Aaron who saved their baby brother at the Nile and sang God's praises on freedom's side of the Red Sea (Exod. 15:19–21). I, *Devorah bat Michael*, am a descendant of women who offered up their mirrors of vanity for the sake of the sanctuary (Exod. 38:8). I am descended from the women who ministered at the entrance to the tabernacle, assisting the priests in the work of the sanctuary.* And I am a descendant of the women who lifted voices and instruments to stir up worship among God's people in the wilderness (Ezra 2:1, 65; Neh. 7:67).[16]

I am also a descendant of the ones who lifted their voices and instruments more than a thousand years later. It was then that Adonai had, at long last, established the place on earth where He "chooses to make His name abide" (Deut. 12:11 NKJV). Solomon's magnificent Temple sprouted from the top of Jerusalem's hill, a brilliant beacon drawing God's pilgrims from far and wide. And in the shadow of that magnificent structure—designed by God, planned by David, and built by Solomon—the Levite musicians stood atop the courtyard platform each and every morning to welcome the day in song.[17]

How incredible it must have been to stand beside the bronze altar and lead worship—even if just for one day out of their whole life—when a Levite musician's group was called to Jerusalem!** Not that leading worship in their local synagogues wasn't a beautiful, weighty privilege. But neither their five years of training nor their time in local ministry could have possibly prepared them for the thrill of Jerusalem's platform.[18]

*"The verb translated 'minister' is rare and interesting, and is used in only one other place of women in the service of the sanctuary (1 Samuel 2:22). It really means 'organized in bands for war,' but it is used of ordinary Levitical service (Numbers 4:23, etc.)." Robert Alan Cole, *Exodus: An Introduction and Commentary* (Inter-Varsity Press, 1973), 236.

**The Levite musicians served on rotations at the Temple as did other descendants of Aaron, including those—like Zechariah—who were chosen to offer the holy incense (see Luke 1:8–9; The Temple Institute, *A Day*).

There they would stand, shoulder to shoulder with as many vocalists as could possibly fit on the three risers that made up the platform.[19] Even Levite children were invited to sing along with them.[20] Standing on the ground around the platform, the youngsters' heads just barely reached the feet of the grown-ups.

Accompanying the vocalists were sacred instruments—*lots* of instruments. This only seems right, since King David—the one who sang and danced in the streets to the strains of lyres and harps and cymbals—is the one who first established the Jerusalem choir (2 Sam. 6:5; 1 Chron. 15:16–22). How breathtaking it would have been for him to stand in the Temple courts built by his son Solomon while being led in song by the choir he founded! King David surely would have wept with joy as their waves of worship billowed over him, the melodies, harmonies, and minor-key threads cascading throughout the city.

The Levites' music actually reached well beyond Jerusalem. The sound of the cymbal and the song of the Levites could be heard in Jericho, some fifteen miles to the northeast, and at the Dead Sea, twenty miles to the southeast.[21] That's actually not hard to believe, because there was no limit placed on the number of vocalists singing in the choir at any one time. As for the band, there could be as many as 12 flutes, 6 lyres, 120 trumpets, and an unlimited number of harps. *Unlimited harps*? How wondrous! And all of this was punctuated by the sound of a single set of copper cymbals.[22] It was the only percussive instrument allowed, and its role was to call people to worship or mark pauses in the music, rather than be part of it. The reason, some said, is that Temple worship was meant to rise to heaven, not rumble the ground.[23]

Even on sparse days—maybe during the quiet, feastless months of summer—the skeleton crew gracing the stage was larger than the worship team of most modern congregations. At the very least, there were to be twelve vocalists accompanied by no less than two flutes, two lyres, two trumpets, and nine harps, plus the one pair of cymbals. But whether by a skeleton crew or full strength, the Levites' praises swept up from the Temple court, through Jerusalem's streets, and over the Judean hills every day. Always moving upward and outward.

The Levite musicians welcomed every morning in the very same way. Selecting their instruments from the two storage rooms beneath the upper courtyard, the musicians assembled with the vocalists at the platform.[24] There they would wait for the unmistakable sound of metal striking stone: the ritual tossing of the *magrefeh* shovel. With the altar's ashes swept and scooped away, the shovel hitting the ground between the sanctuary and the altar signaled the completion of the morning sacrifice.[25] The clatter was so loud that it brought all conversation in Jerusalem to a momentary halt.[26] This dramatic ritual was a passing of the worship baton—or shovel, as it were—from the priests to the musicians. It also served as a deafening last call that bounced off all the stone in the complex. Any musician who had somehow missed the earlier summoning of the cymbal now quickly scurried to the platform.[27]

Praises would then engulf the Temple Mount as the Levites and the worshipers launched into song, welcoming the morning with the *shir shel yom*, the "song of the day."[28] Each day of the week always began with its own designated hymn—the very same daily psalms sung to this day. Six of the psalms celebrate God's six days of creation, and on the Sabbath, the seventh psalm celebrates His rest.* Of course, the Levites didn't sing only those psalms, nor did they always lead from this perch on the packed platform. At other times—including during the pilgrimage feasts—the worship team shifted forward, filling the fifteen steps connecting the Temple courtyard with the Court of Women.[29] No longer concealed within the inner courtyard, the

*Sunday: Psalm 24; Monday: Psalm 48; Tuesday: Psalm 82; Wednesday: Psalm 94; Thursday: Psalm 81; Friday: Psalm 93; Shabbat/Saturday: Psalm 92.

musicians took their places, facing outward instead of toward the place of sacrifice. Ancient rabbis said the semicircular steps under their feet looked like the stone slabs of a threshing floor.[30] Maybe the shape was purely for design and acoustics; it certainly allowed the music to ripple out in all directions. But it must also have brought to mind the original foundation underneath the Temple itself: the threshing floor of Araunah the Jebusite, purchased by King David for just this purpose (2 Sam. 24:18–24).

From those sacred, rounded steps, worship-filled arias radiated outward in all directions. It was a feast for the eyes as much as the ears. The musicians now stood in plain sight, dressed in all their choral regalia. Their praises cascaded over the city as their instruments glinted and gleamed in the sun. Behind them, the bronze doors of the Nicanor Gate soared more than four hundred feet overhead.[31] Its intricately carved metal reflected and refracted sunlight all around the musicians, the rays alighting on the worshipers standing shoulder to shoulder. In those moments of worship there at the Temple, music and light and the scent of holy incense enveloped God's people. Every sense was engaged in the presence and worship of glory.

This otherworldly worship on the fifteen steps marked special moments. One of the most magnificent worship sets sung there was a collection of fifteen psalms. They were sung, some say, at fifteen ascending pitches from one song to the next.[32] These songs made up the most ancient of hymnals, the earliest grouping of psalms discovered bundled together.[33] Written by lyricists, both renowned and unknown, these fifteen psalms are filled with stanzas of soaring praises and brutal lament. And the song book's title? It was called, quite fittingly, the "Songs of the Stairway." To be completely accurate, though, it goes by a lot of different names, depending on who is describing it: the Gradual Psalms, the Songs of Degrees, Songs for Going Up to Worship,

Pilgrim Songs, and even the very simple Fifteen Songs. Today, we probably know them best as the Psalms of Ascent.*

It is thought that Ezra himself grouped these fifteen psalms together as a songbook for the exiles, singing them not only in the sorrow of Babylon's exile, but also on their long-awaited return to Jerusalem.[34] *Glory*. What a triumph for the Levites to eventually be able to sing these psalms on the Temple's rebuilt steps! The simple act of singing on those restored steps testified to God's faithfulness, with each Psalm of Ascent serving as a victory chant. The God of heaven had brought Israel out from the despair of exile into the joy of Jerusalem, rescuing and redeeming as He had done over and over again. Everything around them—the magnificent Temple, the massive courts, those fifteen steps—all served as enormous Ebenezer stones calling out: *See what our God has done!*

I wonder how many smaller Ebenezer stones were scattered along the pilgrimage routes to Jerusalem. Probably more than we could possibly count. So many people, over so many years, made so many journeys to Jerusalem. And amazingly, as God's people answered Jerusalem's call for feast after feast, they—like the Levites at the Temple—also sang from Ezra's hymnal. The Levites may have been Israel's official ministers of music, but the hundreds of thousands of God-fearing Jews making their way to Jerusalem sang the same sacred setlist. They sang the Psalms of Ascent on a loop, from the day they set out from all their scattered points of departure until their eventual reunion in the Temple courts. All along the way, the pilgrims channeled the exiles' anticipation and longing as they, too, answered Jerusalem's call back home.

*You'll find excerpts from these psalms at the beginning of each chapter of this book—a nod to the pilgrimage as we pilgrimage through the feasts. But in this chapter, we're taking the fifteen together, thinking about the pilgrimage psalter as a whole.

This musical tradition turned all of God's children into worship leaders on the pilgrimage roads, placing one foot in front of the other to the tune of the psalms. Together they sang about God, to God, with other people of God. They poured their voices into verses that soared horizontally and reached out vertically. The pilgrims were, as people like to say, preaching truth to themselves and also to one another. They sang truths about the human experience and about the God who answered, and who still answers today. Onward they traveled, united in song and in spirit with the musicians in Jerusalem as the distance between them shrank with every step. The Levites sang from the splendor of the Temple accompanied by sacred instruments. The pilgrims sang from the dusty roads accompanied by children's voices. Each a holy offering.

For the pilgrims, that holy offering, those sacred Songs for Going Up to Worship, were also an excellent playlist for family road trips. Each of the fifteen psalms is short—averaging fewer than seven verses—and focused around one word or word picture. There is also plenty of repetition, making it easy for children to learn and remember. Singing the Psalms of Ascent together was, I think, the purest of Bible memorization plans. Parents and grandparents, aunts and uncles, children and cousins were proclaiming truth each day as they rose up and lay down and walked along the way, living out Deuteronomy 6 as they propelled each other closer to the presence of God.**

Despite their simplicity, Ezra's collection of these particular psalms offered a depth and richness for people on pilgrimage, because the lyrics themselves travel a pilgrimage, both spiritually and geographically. The hymnal moved pilgrims through words of lament, thanksgiving, wisdom, and praise. It is a lyrical journey that begins with David's cry from the fringes

**"Repeat them to your children. Talk about them when you sit in your house and when you walk along the road, when you lie down and when you get up" (Deut. 6:7 CSB).

of geography and faith in Psalm 120 and that ends with the joy of worshiping in Jerusalem's courts in Psalm 134. As such, Ezra's collection is as much a treasure map as it is a songbook, guiding people ever closer to the living God in spirit and in space.

The dotted lines of this treasure map—each individual psalm in the Psalter—directed hearts toward hope. Whether expressing joy or lament, each of the fifteen psalms captures the reason that God's people were on pilgrimage in the first place: the certain hope that the Almighty hears our cries, protects our steps, redeems our pain, and leads us to Himself. Even Ezra's decision to begin the hymnal with David's lament of lying lips and enemy arrows reminds us of why we *all* need to embark on a journey toward God's presence. We need to ascend with hearts and feet toward God's throne because we all dwell in broken, far-off places. Even in those distant places, the verses remind us that God is still near, and He calls us to lift our eyes and draw ever nearer. So the pilgrims looked up. They lifted their eyes toward the hill, and toward the Rescuer who dwelled there.

Along the way, the pilgrims were reminded that they were living out the very words they sang. They, too, trudged beneath the noonday sun and shivered under the midnight moon. They, too, felt God keep their feet from slipping when their legs grew heavy. They faced opposition from enemies along the way, occupiers who hated the God of Zion. They, too, felt God's blessing anoint them as they joined with new travelers at each juncture, living out unity on the pilgrimage roads. With increasing volume and anticipation, the ever-growing pilgrim choir proclaimed God's goodness on the roads ascending toward Jerusalem.*

Eventually, the pilgrims drew close enough to hear their own voices mingling with the song of the Levites, their shared

*It's really no wonder that Mary and Joseph lost track of Jesus on the road home from Jerusalem. More incredible is that it didn't happen every single time amid this multigenerational, multinational parade of worship and fellowship!

refrains bridging the dwindling distance. Oh, how that sound must have quickened their hearts and their steps, hastening them ever closer to the Temple of *Hashem*, "the Name." Finally catching sight of the sanctuary in all its glory must have stopped them in their tracks, with the sun lighting up every bit of marble and stone and gold and brass. The surge of adrenaline at the sight of that splendor would propel them up the final ascent.

Walking within the city walls, at long last, the weary yet wonder-filled travelers would make their way to the Temple complex with their children and supplies in tow. On the way to evening worship, people reunited with family and friends, awash in the rays of the setting sun and the music of the Levite choir. Together they experienced the fulfillment of every word they had been singing since their journeys to Jerusalem first began. And together, they were now singing those very same psalms with the accompaniment of the sacred instruments. Standing shoulder to shoulder, the pilgrims were finally able to "lift up [their] hands in the sanctuary and bless the Lord"—the promise of that final Psalm of Ascent (Ps. 134:2).

There was, however, one Psalm of Ascent left unfulfilled for a very long time:

> There I will make a horn sprout up for David.
> I will prepare a lamp for my anointed one. . . .
> The crown on my anointed one will shine.
>
> (Ps. 132:17–18 GW)

Three times each year, throughout the Judean countryside, the pilgrims proclaimed *en masse* God's promise of the Messiah, the Anointed One. It was a melody of redemption rippling across the Land, even from the lips of the holy family. I wonder what it was like for Mary and Joseph to sing those words alongside loved ones and strangers during their walks from Nazareth to Jerusalem. Did her voice catch and his eyes overflow as they watched their boy, first toddling, then skipping, then striding toward Jerusalem as He grew? And what was it like for Jesus? Did He sing those words right along with them? He, the Word made flesh, singing about *Himself*? What could have consumed His thoughts and emotions every time His ears flooded with the voices of His companions expressing a deep longing for the King's presence and rescue?

He listened to them long for Jerusalem, the very place where Jesus knew He *would* rescue them all one day. He also knew that He would rescue them, and us, while wearing a crown that would not shine but pierce. It is too great for us to fathom. Yet Jesus continued to walk, to sing, and to fellowship along those ascending pilgrimage roads, feast after feast, year after year, crowd after crowd, psalm after psalm. There in the Temple courts, Jesus raised His hands in the sanctuary alongside the rest of the pilgrims and blessed the Father, *His* Father.

As the instruments' last notes hung suspended in Jerusalem's evening air, one of the priests would step forward, raising his hands toward the pilgrims. He blessed God's people with words from the wilderness, pronouncing the benediction that God shared with Aaron in Sinai's desert, to be repeated by his descendants over God's children for generation after generation:

> May the Lord bless you and protect you;
> may the Lord make his face shine on you and be
> gracious to you;
> may the Lord look with favor on you and give
> you peace.
>
> (Num. 6:24–26 CSB)

Receiving Aaron's blessing there at the steps of the Temple evoked profound emotion in God's people, as individuals and families and as a nation. Joy and thanksgiving rose in response to God's tender words for their flourishing, protection, provision, and peace. Not only for their future, but as a remembrance and celebration that God had just delivered on all those very things. God had indeed blessed and kept them along the dangerous pilgrimage roads. Adonai had shown kindness by surrounding them with loved ones along the way. He had been gracious through the generous brethren in Jerusalem. God had shined His face upon them and brought them His peace, for they now stood before His presence in the city called the City of Peace, the City of Shalom: *Jeru-shalem.** Their hearts must have swelled with gratitude.

I wonder what filled Jesus's heart in those moments of blessing. After all, Aaron's benediction was spoken over Jesus, too. What was it like for the immortal Great High Priest to be blessed by one of the mortal priests He had knit together in the womb? The words of that ancient blessing communicated something altogether different as they fell on the Messiah. Perhaps they encouraged Jesus, reminding Him that whether He was teaching, healing, or sharing a meal, the Father's face always shone on Him, always favored Him (Luke 2:52). Through early morning prayers in solitary places, the grace and peace of heaven sustained Him through a mission no one else could grasp. From the weapons of words, nails, and death, the Father would bless and keep Jesus in ways no one else could fathom. Indeed, the priestly blessing filled and fell on Jesus with realities that not even the priests pronouncing the words could comprehend. Yet Jesus received them. He received the priestly blessing in Jerusalem, in Nazareth, and in every synagogue He entered—just like the rest of His people did, and just like His people do even now.

*With regard to the translation of Jerusalem, there are varying interpretations about the meaning of *Jeru*; the most common are "possession," "the Lord will provide," and "foundation." There is no dispute about *salem*, the root of *shalom*: to be at peace, whole, and complete. In all cases, the combination of Jeru-salem points to the wholeness and peace that come from God. Hence, the common title, City of Peace.

Whether spoken from the *bema* of synagogues or the pulpits of churches, the words that God placed in Aaron's mouth continue to pour out on people created in God's image. Indeed, in the moments when we struggle to know what God wants for us, we can look to these verses. They are an anchor for our souls whether we are wounded or full of wonder, feeling hopeless or hope-filled. They reorient us to the enduring gifts that the Giver wants to give us and that He is exceedingly able to give. In that sense, the priestly blessing is so much like the Lord's Prayer: God giving us words to ask Him for the very things He is already holding in His open, outstretched hands. Gifts and graces He loves to give.

Sometimes even now, when our pastors speak the priestly blessing over us at the end of worship, I think about my forefather Aaron pronouncing those very same words over my ancestors in the desert. It fills me with both the freedom of promise and the weight of purpose. And, in those moments, I also think about my grandfather. I imagine what it would have been like to have him, with his priestly lineage woven into his love for me, rest his hands on my shoulders and pray those same ancient words. I can almost hear him asking Adonai to bless me and protect me, to be kind and gracious to me, to shine His face upon me, and to give me shalom. Certainly, Adonai has done all these things for me in all the ways that truly matter: His redemption, His intercession, His abiding presence. Indeed, He has done all these things for all of us, whether born into the vine or grafted in.

Jerusalem calls us to receive.

CHAPTER 4

Temporary Shelter

The LORD will guard you from all harm; He will guard your life.

Psalm 121:7 Tanakh Translation

My childhood synagogue sat at the edge of a cornfield. That isn't too surprising, really, when you consider that cornfields cover more than one-third of Iowa.[35] For a decade of my life, those farms put food on our dinner tables and ethanol in our gas tanks. And one summer, an Iowa cornfield also became my first official jobsite. At fourteen, I had discovered that I was too low on the employment totem pole to get a job at any establishment equipped with air-conditioning. Hearing of my predicament, a classmate told me about an awesome gig: detasseling corn. (If you grew up in Iowa, you are already groaning.) In the moment, it seemed like the answer to all my unreasonable teenage demands: no weekends, no evenings, and no long-term commitment.

In theory, detasseling was a great job for an early-rising introvert like myself. I simply had to board a repurposed school bus in the Walmart parking lot at 5:30 AM and let it carry me and my co-laborers to a designated farm. The work itself, said my classmate, was to walk up and down the neatly planted rows until early afternoon. What he hadn't told me was that, as we trekked through the seemingly endless rows of corn under the blazing summer sun, we were to pull the tassel from the top of each cornstalk in every fifth row. It's all about cross-pollination. Honestly, just thinking about it now still makes me tired.

My parents were all in favor of me doing some manual labor. So they gave me their blessing and sent me off with a sack lunch and an insulated thermos. If only my wardrobe had been as well-suited as my provisions. Instead, wanting to look cute for my first day of work, I headed to the meetup spot dressed in a bright ensemble from the ESPRIT store: crisp yellow shorts and a sleeveless white top adorned with multicolored polka dots. My new coworkers—dressed in long sleeves and Wrangler jeans—greeted me with raised eyebrows and a few smirks. Apparently, native Iowans know better than to show up for farm work dressed like a giant bag of Skittles.

By the end of the first day, I was coated with sweat, dirt, and a little blood. I had learned the hard way what my coworkers already knew: It was very unwise to walk through a field of razor-sharp leaves with bare arms and legs. I did *not* make the same mistake the following day. I was, however, just as miserable. Not only did I wear long sleeves and long pants, but I also donned the farm-issued black trash bag that served as a poncho. This kindness was meant to keep us dry from the nighttime rain still clinging to the broad leaves. But I very quickly concluded that the plastic bag was a horrible idea, unless I wanted to work inside my own personal, mobile sauna—which I did not. All day, we each worked alone with our thoughts, without the distraction of smartphones or earbuds. I didn't even own a Sony Walkman.

It's no shock that I didn't last a full week. I don't remember if I even got paid. What I do remember is crumpling into a heap of fatigue-induced sobs on our basement stairway for no apparent reason and being physically unable to stop. I may have run high school track and abused my feet through a decade of ballet, but I proved to be no match for this Midwestern rite of passage.

You might think that I never wanted anything to do with an Iowa cornfield ever again. I'm sure I cried those very words to my mom as she got down and wrapped me up in her arms. But I didn't really mean it. Incredibly, I still found something soothing in those perfect, lush rows that stretched endlessly over the horizon. I can't count the number of times I pulled over on the highway during my summers home from college just to snap photos of those vast cornfields. Whether the stalks swayed under a coral sky at dawn or the green hue of a storm front at dusk, the beauty of Iowa's landscape mesmerized me.

The fact that our tiny synagogue rested at the edge of a cornfield only deepened my affection for them, especially during Sukkot, the Feast of Booths. Each autumn, in anticipation of the seven-day festival, our congregation assembled outside to build the requisite makeshift shelter against the backdrop of that field. The corn had long since been harvested by then, so the ground was nothing but crisp, brown stubble. But the charm remained. We spent hours laughing together in the October chill while tying yarn around the stems of apples and pears and wrapping twine around long-necked gourds and dried ears of corn. Eventually, our autumnal bounty hung from every branch of the shelter's thatched roof and all three of its wobbly walls.

I can't say whether God's people farmed corn in ancient Israel. No one really knows what kind of grains *dagan* or *shibolet* actually were. But when I spent those autumn days decorating our sukkah by the cornfield, I liked to imagine that my ancestors farmed those same stately rows.[36] I felt rooted there, and not just because it was the landscape of my youth. Huddling with our congregation inside that three-sided shelter cultivated a deep sense of connection to my people. I felt connected to my Jewish brethren all around the globe who were—at that very same moment—chatting or eating or sleeping in their own little booths. I felt joined to our ancestors, who pilgrimaged to Jerusalem and lived in their shelters side by side for the whole week. And I felt tethered to our even more ancient ancestors who dwelled in the desert wilderness. Their sojourn is the whole reason for the booths in the first place.

> You are to celebrate-it-as pilgrimage, a pilgrimage-
>   festival to YHWH, for seven days a year—
> a law for the ages, throughout your generations:
> in the seventh New-Moon you are to
>   celebrate-it-as-pilgrimage—
> in huts you are to stay for seven days, every native in
>   Israel is to stay in huts—
> in order that your generations may know that in huts I
>   had the Children of Israel stay
> when I brought them out of the land of Egypt, I am
>   YHWH your God!
>
> (Lev. 23:41–43 The Schocken Bible)[37]

God's intention for our time in rickety shelters is to help us remember the Israelites' trek through the wilderness. It is meant to connect our hands, feet, hearts, and minds to the daily intimacy they experienced with God in those years after the deliverance from Egypt. It allows us to sample a taste of their utter dependence on His sheltering and sustenance through the desert. Interestingly, Jewish tradition teaches that the Feast of Booths begins on the anniversary of when the Shekinah first swept up into the sky to guide them by the pillars of cloud and fire. As we remember all of these things, the Feast of Booths is an annual invitation to meditate on the Israelites' absolute need for God and on His unrelenting faithfulness to them. It's also an invitation for us to grow deeper in our own understanding that we, too, need God for everything and that He is faithful to provide.

But God's command to live in temporary huts to commemorate the wilderness sojourn was a curious thing for its initial audience. After all, when God said to dwell in huts for a week to recall the forty years of wandering, the Israelites were, in fact, still wandering and, therefore, still living in huts. The original recipients of that Feast of Booths command didn't need to remember the days of transient living, because they were still living them! They felt the fatigue of constantly raising walls they would have to take right back down in a matter of months, weeks, or days. They felt the chill of sleeping under ceilings that fluttered in the summer wind and leaked in the winter rain. They felt the sweat of gathering new building supplies as the desert took its toll. And they bore the physical weight of it all every single time they pulled up stakes to follow wherever the cloud of glory led.

All of the people in all of the narratives from the exodus in Egypt to the other side of the Jordan knew intimately what it meant to live in temporary shelters. And yet here was God, talking about those shelters in the past tense. His words were merciful and beautiful because, just like the larger pilgrimage command, this one cradled a tender promise. It was a promise that, one day, their refugee years would be in the past. It was a promise that they would one day be able to set down roots. It was a promise that they—and all the generations after them—would have to actually stop and take time to remember what it was like to wander without a place to call home and to remember it with their whole bodies.

That is what biblical remembering is, after all. Not simply considering with our minds, but remembering with arms and legs, with sight and smell. That's the purpose of this annual festal encampment: to engage in tactile remembrance of those nomadic days. God knew that when His children finally planted their feet in the Promised Land, they might forget their reliance on Him. No longer wanderers, they might grow accustomed to living in stone cities surrounded by fortified walls. With the wilderness a distant memory, they might start thinking that their good fortune was entirely the work of their own hands. And maybe they would even begin to forget the One who had rescued them with His mighty outstretched arm from their suffering in Egypt.

So God gave Israel the Feast of Booths as a gift, a sort of annual fall retreat. Creation itself would serve as the retreat center, where every family would dwell outdoors for the week, exposed to the natural elements and separated from creature comforts. The feast puts us in a position to feel the wind, smell the rain, and see the stars in community. It's an opportunity to taste the trust of our ancestors, thereby renewing our own. Through it, we are able to claim afresh the God of the wilderness, the One who proved Himself o'er and o'er.

Throughout those forty years of wandering, the Israelites carried God's promise of the Feast of Booths along with them, lightening their load emotionally, if not yet physically. Then, finally in Canaan, the exodus wanderers took all of this remembering to heart. They treasured it so deeply that, by the time of Solomon, the Feast of Booths was known simply as *HaGag*: "the Feast" or "the Festival."[38] Even gentiles understood that, aside from Shabbat, Sukkot was the most important Jewish festival, the festival par excellence.[39] And it *was* quite a sight: the whole nation of Israel arriving in Jerusalem each fall, setting up their makeshift booths all over Mount Zion's hill. Even their temporary village built around the sanctuary was a remembering of sorts: a harkening back to when the twelve tribes camped in formation around the tabernacle within their little tents in the wilderness. Securely settled in the Promised Land as promised, the nation of Israel built their commemorative booths year after year, remembering and celebrating together. It was, indeed, *Z'man Simchateinu*, the "season of our joy"—a nickname for the Feast of Booths even to this day.

It's no wonder that Solomon chose to dedicate the magnificent new Temple during this pilgrimage festival. All of Israel would be there to celebrate together. Finally, more than five hundred years after Israel crossed the Jordan, God, too, had a permanent place on earth to dwell. That historic week in Jerusalem, Solomon and all of God's people lived in their makeshift shelters, remembering His protection and provision in the desert. And, gathered around the Temple complex, all of those descendants of the wilderness wanderers looked on as the same divine cloud of glory swept into the Holy of Holies, taking up residence in the gilded cedar chamber (1 Kings 8:10–13). Surely that glimpse of the Shekinah remained seared in their memories all the days of their lives.

Unfortunately, the lesson of the booths did not last. The nation drifted into trusting the solutions of their own wisdom, their own leadership, and their own traditions—the very things from which God was trying to protect them. And so, four hundred years after the dedication of Solomon's sanctuary, Babylon pulled down the fortified walls of Jerusalem and left the city smoldering. The once-glorious Temple lay in ruins at the hands of Nebuchadnezzar's army, the fallout of Israel's own rebellion.

Once again, God's people became exiles, living as foreigners in the land of Babylon. There they dwelled under the oppression of "Zion haters," as the psalmist lamented in Psalm 129. Maybe that's why Ezra selected that particular hymn as one of the Psalms of Ascent, his exilic songbook. The lyrics of Psalm 129 became a defiant cry against the oppression and torture of Babylon: "They have greatly oppressed me from my youth, but they have not gained the victory over me" (Ps. 129:2).

After seventy years, that verse rang out like a victory chant along the desert roads as the first wave of exiles finally marched back to Jerusalem with Cyrus's freedom papers in hand. Just as God had promised (Jer. 29:10).

Jerusalem, though she lay in ruins, was a beautiful sight for exile eyes. As they settled in, the returnees gathered together inside Nehemiah's rebuilt walls in front of the Water Gate. There they listened to Ezra read to them the Torah, the Five Books of Moses. All of them—every man, woman, and child who could understand—listened to God's words, beginning with "In the beginning . . ." (Gen. 1:1). But then everything came to a halt on just the second day of reading, when Ezra reached God's instructions for the Feast of Booths, near the end of Leviticus. The feast, they all realized, was less than two weeks away. So the people got up and scattered to the hills, gathering leafy limbs of olive, pine, myrtle, and palm. They built their shelters on mended roofs, in reconstructed courts, and at the Water Gate, physically remembering Israel's nomad years in the desert. They remembered God's protection of their ancestors on the way to the Promised Land and of themselves on their own return from Babylon. The exiles were finally home, regardless of the rubble around them, able to answer Jerusalem's call again (Neh. 8:17). *Z'man Simchateinu*, the season of our joy, took on an even richer meaning for God's people that year.

It is said that the three walls and roof of the sukkah are like the arm of God, wrapping around His people, cradling us when we rest within them.[40] Certainly, it must have felt that way to the returning exiles, as they spent the entire week of that Feast of Booths listening to God's words all day and then sleeping in His embrace—the booths—all night. It likely felt that way to every pilgrim who *ever* gathered in Jerusalem to celebrate the feast. Together they all experienced God's embrace as they settled into makeshift shelters on Jerusalem's hill, beholding the very same stars that their ancestors beheld through each of their rickety roofs.

Of course, before beholding the stars, there had to be the building of booths. And so, pouring into Jerusalem the day before the feast began, the pilgrims scouted out their spots and reunited with relatives and friends as the city swelled.[41] Even Jerusalem's year-round residents spilled out onto the streets to set up temporary home sites for the feast. These thousands of families pitched camp on Mount Zion, their shelters all nestled within a radius of three-quarters of a mile of the sanctuary complex.[42] This distance, a "Sabbath-day's journey," kept everyone close enough to walk to the Temple on Shabbat.[43] Shelters stood upon rooftops and roadways, in courtyards and gardens, filling every square inch of available space.

By the end of that day, the eve of the feast, a lush patchwork of leafy roofs blanketed Mount Zion, creating a vastly different bird's-eye view than the rest of the year, when the roofs of the rich and royal were easily distinguishable from those of the poor and common. Indeed, this is one of the most beautiful realities of the Feast of Booths: It brought about a leveling of the mountains and valleys of humanity. The ancient rabbis even developed construction guidelines for the temporary shelters to ensure that God's people remained equally vulnerable toward Him and one another. Everyone's roofs could be thatched tightly enough to provide shade during the heat of the day yet must still be loose enough to see the stars through them at night. The three walls of every booth—that loving embrace of the Lord—had to be fashioned from unfinished branches, vines, or twigs. Anything grown from the ground but no longer rooted was fit to use.[44]

The philosophy behind all these construction guidelines, the details of which fill volumes, flows from God's use of the word *sukkah* (booth) instead of *mishkan* (tabernacle). One is small, temporary, and draped with branches, while the other is majestic, lasting, and draped with splendor. God's choice of words meant everything. This was no Feast of *Tabernacles*. This was a feast of simplicity, humility, and vulnerability. And so, on that booth construction day, the air filled with the sounds of everyone—young and old, rich and poor—hoisting branches, joining walls, and instructing little helpers. Countless hands, tools, and branches connected people on Mount Zion to one another and to their refugee forebears in the exodus wilderness.

The whole thing sounds refreshing to me, even romantic. Especially on sunny, breezy days and clear, autumn nights. Of course, when the rains fell on all those loosely thatched roofs, it must have been a very different story. And, since the Feast of Booths takes place at the beginning of Israel's rainy season, a downpour was always a distinct possibility—and still is for modern-day sukkah dwellers! But despite the threat of foul weather, the Feast of Booths remained *Z'man Simchateinu*, the season of our joy, because every moment—whether sunny or rainy—connects God's people to the wilderness wandering and to the God who sustains in every season and circumstance. A week of sukkah living is a reminder of God's kept promises, which are our only trustworthy shelter.

As the sun began to set on the mass construction project, trumpets would sound from the Temple Mount, announcing the advent of the feast. Music settled over the endless sea of leafy booths, including the one that sheltered the head of the Messiah. How many times did young Jesus gather branches with His brothers, scampering around the Mount of Olives with shouts of laughter? Did He, too, sense the embrace of the Father—*His* Father—when He broke bread with loved ones inside the three walls of their sukkah? How many nights did Jesus gaze up at the stars through the roof with His mother? I wonder if the beauty and weight of it all overwhelmed Mary at times. Maybe she marveled that the divine One dwelling in their makeshift hut once dwelled within her. Perhaps she pondered the mystery that

Jesus was not simply dwelling for a week inside their temporary booth of branches, but that He was the fullness of heaven living inside a temporary tent of flesh. Glory was contained and constrained in ways we cannot begin to grasp.

In the end, Jesus's temporary tent was only meant to last for thirty-three years. And as that time ticked away, He experienced so many "lasts," including a last Feast of Booths. That year, Jesus chose not to take part in building a shelter. He didn't even pilgrimage to Jerusalem along with family or friends (John 7:8–10). Instead, by the time Jesus quietly arrived, construction was probably complete. Maybe the echoes of the last trumpet blasts were wafting over the roads when He finally ascended Jerusalem's hill and took in the patchwork of shelters blanketing the mountain. Maybe He chose to go alone that year because He knew it would be His last view of the Temple Mount adorned with booths, their vines still green and branches still fresh. Maybe Jesus wanted a quiet moment to take it all in.

That verdant quilt of makeshift shelters spoke a sort of parable for Jesus's entire mortal life. No one's shelter was more humble than His, because He—the Light of the entire World—was dwelling inside a vulnerable human body. And soon, just like the thatched roofs that couldn't keep out the rain, the Messiah's mortal covering wouldn't be able to shelter Him from the barbs of words and stings of whips that would rain down on Him. It wasn't meant to, though. Jesus had always intended to give up His own body to cover ours. He had always planned to exchange the temporary for the eternal—not only beyond His own grave but beyond ours as well.

Jesus's entire mission was to make a way for us to join Him in a place where we will live sustained by His glorious presence. That future dwelling place is not humble or flimsy, but magnificent and unshakeable. And God will dwell there with His people, not in a cloudy pillar above our heads but on the throne in our midst. That will be our true, enduring *Z'man Simchateinu*. An eternal season of joy.

> For seven days celebrate the festival to the LORD
> your God
> at the place the LORD will choose. . . . And your joy will
> be complete.
>
> (Deut. 16:15 NIV)

While we wait for those days of eternity, the Feast of Booths is meant to give us a foretaste of complete joy. It reminds the nation of Israel—both natural and grafted in—to trust and rely on God instead of the works of our own hands. The booths invite us to rest each day in His everlasting embrace. To abide in God's love while abiding in our vulnerable bodies.

My homemade booths these days are small affairs, set up next to the fig tree in my backyard and held together with zip ties. I don't live and eat and sleep in them all week like my forebears did or like my brethren still do in Orthodox communities. But throughout each day of the feast, I pause to contemplate my sukkah in all its simplicity. I make time to step out into the crisp autumn air and breathe it in. I sit for a spell, letting the sunlight spill through the branches over my head. I snack on an apple or a pear or some homemade pumpkin challah.

Through it all, I am reminded that the everyday rhythms of life provide beautiful opportunities to learn and live the lessons of the booths. The sukkah teaches me about trust and joy in the middle of rote routine and unexpected downpours—just like the generation of Israelites who lived in temporary desert homes and like the centuries of pilgrims who spent a week every year in booths on Jerusalem's hill.

When I rest inside my own little shelter, adorned with gourds and apples and—yes—dried cobs of corn, I take in God's creation and remember His faithfulness. I close my eyes within the three wobbly walls and remember that the divine embrace wraps around me with a mighty outstretched arm and a nail-pierced hand. I allow Him to reassure me that His divine embrace is a forever shelter, magnificent and immoveable, regardless of the storms I weather along the pilgrimage path. *That* is our enduring *Z'man Simchateinu*, the season of our joy for eternity.

Jerusalem calls us to abide.

CHAPTER 5

Shaking Faith

To You, enthroned in heaven, I lift my eyes.
Psalm 123:1 JPS85

As a Jewish kid, my very favorite day in synagogue was the celebration of Queen Esther and her cousin Mordechai. I loved that our Midwestern celebration had roots reaching all the way back to ancient Persia, to the dramatic moments when God delivered His chosen people from Haman's genocidal plan. That divine rescue, first celebrated twenty-five hundred years ago, has been commemorated by worshipful hearts in grateful communities every single year since. Of course, world history has provided ample opportunities for the Jewish people to remember suffering and deliverance. So recounting the long thread of oppression and salvation—both before and since the Persian rescue—is also now stitched into many modern-day Purim celebrations.

Honestly, though, it wasn't the rescue that inspired me to circle the date on my Hello Kitty calendar as a child. It was the party. Most Jewish kids will admit the same thing, because when it comes to celebrating the rescue from Haman, congregations all around the globe follow the same spirited template: a reading of the scroll of Esther in the sanctuary followed by costumed parades and carnival games. It's a pattern that binds us together across cultures and continents in worship and in merriment. It is *commanded*, after all. Mordechai's letter to the Jews living in exile throughout the Persian Empire declared that the anniversary of this national redemption should "never fail to be remembered and celebrated throughout every generation" (Esther 9:28). So, celebrate we do! And celebrate we did, in my cozy little synagogue at the edge of a cornfield.

Gathered in the sanctuary, the whole congregation paid rapt attention to the dramatic retelling of Mordechai and Esther, as is done in every synagogue. Together, we drowned out every single utterance of Haman's name with our vast array of homemade and store-bought noisemakers or, for the empty-handed, with boos and jeers. We kids would parade around the property like a clone army of Esthers and Mordecais, finally making our way to the synagogue basement, where we were engulfed by the sound of music and the smell of sugar. We tossed rings around bottles and pitched beanbags through holes. We walked for cakes and bobbed for apples. We clamored for seats during musical chairs. And we danced and dunk-tanked. (Okay, my modest congregation didn't have a dunk tank, but a kid can dream, can't she?) All of this revelry, while still decked out in biblical costume. There is no doubt that if you had asked me as a child what the most festive Jewish holiday was, I would have shrieked without hesitation: Purim!*

But I would have been wrong. Purim was not the most festive of Jewish festivals. Not by a long shot. Not while the Temple still stood and pilgrims still journeyed to Jerusalem's

*Purim is Hebrew for "lots," referring to the lots cast by Haman to determine the execution date for all the Jewish people living in Persia.

hill, at least. No, in those days, the most jubilant celebration among God's people was actually the Feast of Booths. Yes, that autumn camping excursion atop Mount Zion. I realize that a week of outdoor living—in shelters hardly weatherproof—may sound like a candidate for the *least* festive, especially if young children are involved. But, in fact, the Feast of Booths was known even among gentiles as the most festive of all the Jewish holidays.[45]

> Be joyful at your festival [the Feast of Booths]—you, your sons and daughters, your male and female servants, and the Levites, the foreigners, the fatherless and the widows who live in your towns. For seven days celebrate the festival to the Lord your God at the place the Lord will choose.
>
> (Deut. 16:14–15 NIV)

The King of Kings commanded a weeklong celebration for the Feast of Booths. And His subjects obeyed—with absolute abandon. Once the task of building the shelters was behind them, the Jerusalem pilgrims embraced the divine assignment of rejoicing for seven straight days and nights. Especially the nights. After the final sacrifice each day, as the golden shimmer of sunset washed over the woven roofs blanketing the city, people of every age and stage and station began stepping into the sights and sounds and smells of *Z'man Simchateinu*, the season of our joy.

Those Feast of Booths sunsets were nothing short of disorienting. Because, instead of becoming gradually draped in darkness, Jerusalem's hillside found itself suddenly bathed in light. Sixteen spectacular flames roared to life in the Temple courtyard in a nightly ritual, unique to the Feast of Booths, known as the "Illumination of the Temple." But the lamps illuminated more than just the Temple; the flames lit up the entire mountain like the noonday sun. Not a single courtyard or alleyway in all of Jerusalem remained in shadows.[46] It's no wonder that gentiles considered the Feast of Booths to be the greatest Jewish feast, because the light radiating from God's mountain could be seen for miles and miles, all night long.

The light poured from four otherworldly lampstands that seemed to sprout like redwoods from the stone courtyard. Each one soared seventy-five feet into the sky. *Seventy-five feet*. That's about six stories. Or, if you've been to Tulsa, Oklahoma, the height of the Golden Driller Statue. But instead of arms resting on a rig that draws oil from the earth, the massive lampstands branched up toward the sky, each one extending four bowls of oil like sixteen toasts to heaven. These golden lightbearers seemed to cry out with sixteen rounds of *L'chaim!—To Life!*—in a toast roaring from the mountain to the Giver of life and light.

Making sure those goblets of fire never ran dry, young priests-in-training served as sacred stewards, refilling the giant bowls of oil throughout the entire night. These lowest-ranking members of the priestly sect clambered to those highest heights, scaling wooden ladders that reached the very top of the lampstands, all the while lugging sixteen-gallon pitchers of olive oil.[47] When they weren't hauling fuel up the wooden rungs, the newbies carried fresh wicks. These were no ordinary twisted strands of thread. The wicks of the Feast of Booths lamps were fashioned from thick strips of worn-out priestly garments, in an ancient system of reuse and recycle. Between replenishing oil and igniting new wicks, the young runners made sure that those larger-than-life torches never went out, not until the sun rose and could resume its job of illuminating God's mountain.

Honestly, my fear of heights kicks in just imagining the young Levites climbing those six-story ladders. But what a view it must have been! Not only of the booths blanketing Mount Zion and the autumn landscape stretching into the distance, but also of the festive scene playing out right below them. Each night, hundreds of thousands of pilgrims frolicked in the light of the roaring flames and the nonstop music of the Levite musicians. They laughed and clapped and sang along as the streets swelled with merriment and the city transformed into a full-scale feast for the senses.

Every single night of the Feast of Booths, from the final sacrifice until the break of the next day, Jerusalem made the carnivals in my synagogue basement look like child's play. Which, to be fair, is what they were. But these fall carnivals on Mount Zion had even the adults shrieking with delight. Most pulled all-nighters throughout the entire weeklong feast, including the Levites and even the great King David.[48] With the sky-high lampstands turning night into day, the feast destroyed everyone's internal clock. Undoubtedly, the thousands of breezy shelters around the Temple Mount served as napping sanctuaries throughout the daytime hours.

This full-throttle celebration had even the scribes and teachers of the Law immersing themselves in the fun. While Levites sang from the fifteen rounded steps, well-respected religious leaders led the people in merriment through the streets. They sang and danced with hymns of praise and burning torches. They tumbled and performed acrobatics of all kinds. And these "pious men of distinction" juggled eight of whatever happened to be on hand, whether eggs, torches, knives, or glasses of wine.[49]

Even the most highly regarded among them led in the hijinks, including the great teacher Gamaliel. A descendant of King David and grandson of the renowned sage Hillel, Gamaliel was known simply as "the Elder" during his longtime leadership of the Sanhedrin. His peers honored him with this title because of his great wisdom and deep love of God.[50] This is the very same Gamaliel that the apostle Paul identified as his teacher, as evidence of his own elite biblical training (Acts 22:3). This same Gamaliel would convince the Sanhedrin to free the apostles rather than put them to death, admonishing them that, if the Jesus movement was of God, there would be nothing they could do to stop it (Acts 5:27–42). This Gamaliel—the serious, scholarly, esteemed Elder—was known to sing with abandon during the Feast of Booths and to not only juggle eight flaming torches but perform handstands on just his two thumbs.[51]

Thinking about the way Paul's mentor celebrated makes me wonder if the apostle, too, had performed in the streets during the feast. Did Gamaliel teach Paul to juggle fire? And what about Jesus? Did Jesus ever juggle goblets of wine, torches of fire, or even just a handful of eggs with His disciples in the streets? Maybe He simply smiled to Himself while watching the silliness of those two men—Gamaliel and Paul—as they celebrated. After all, the Messiah knew they would eventually, in spite of themselves, do so much to advance His ministry of redemption. Either way, it's not hard to imagine young Jesus, His brothers, and their friends juggling anything and everything they could get their little hands on during those annual celebrations. Or to picture them attempting backflips and somersaults through the crowded streets just like their favorite teachers. Surely they must have.

Yet, for all their frivolity, these nightly festivals under the lights weren't the heart of the rejoicing during the feast among the booths:

> And you shall take for yourselves on the first day the fruit of beautiful trees, branches of palm trees, the boughs of leafy trees, and willows of the brook; and you shall rejoice before the LORD your God for seven days.
>
> (Lev. 23:40 NKJV)

For seven days, all of God's people celebrated with bundles of foliage—very *specific* foliage. They rejoiced before Him with the fruit of a citron tree, fronds from palm trees, branches of myrtle, and boughs of willow. What does that even look like?

And *why?* Maybe Moses actually asked these questions as a sidebar while taking the Leviticus dictation from God. But if he did ask, Moses didn't record God's response in writing. He did, however, *teach* it.[52] The ancient practice from pre-Temple days, passed down all the way through Jesus's life and ministry, was the same. In fact, it is still the same today.

Sitting in the shade of their newly built shelters on that first day of the feast, every single pilgrim retreated, fruit and greenery in hand, to follow God's instructions for the most sacred of craft projects. There was no glitter or glue, only these specific supplies straight from the land. On laps, tables, and sandy floors, pilgrims of every age fashioned identical bouquets in a tradition that has passed through the ages: one palm frond, flanked on the right by three small myrtle branches and on the left by two willow boughs, all bound together firmly with an intricate weave of more fresh leaves. Old hands guided young ones. Preadolescent fingers tied and untied in exasperation. Sharp fronds drew blood—kind of like my Iowa cornstalks had, except I had no beauty to show for it, while they did in abundance. The finished product is named for the most prominent piece of the greenery: the palm frond, or *lulav*.

For the entire feast week in Jerusalem, whether people were worshiping, visiting with friends, or checking on the sick, every hand carried a lulav.[53] It was as if the booths and lulavs worked in tandem to remind God's people of the exodus sojourn. While they were gathered inside their shelters, they remembered God's sheltering in the desert. When they walked outside amid the throngs of fellow worshipers, their bouquets of greenery brought back the sights, sounds, and smells of the wilderness terrain:[54] Palms from valley lows, myrtles from mountain heights, and willows of the quenching brook all brought the exodus journey to life in people's arms. The bright yellow citron of abundance was proof that the desert road eventually led to the Land of promise. Whether carried in people's hands or serving as shelter over their heads, God's creation whispered testimonies of His faithfulness during every moment of the feast. The pilgrims could not help but to live and breathe thankfulness there on Mount Zion.

In all their bounteous beauty, the lulavs—just like the make-shift shelters—kept every person on level playing ground in their remembering. Even people who secured the ends of their branches with golden thread—because they either had great means or had scrimped and saved—were required to keep it all literally under wraps. Gilding the inside of the lulav was allowed as an act of personal worship, but only so long as it couldn't be seen.[55] There would be no status or flash found in these objects of worship, only substance: the substance of thanksgiving. Then the Lord said:

> Observe . . . the Festival of Ingathering at the turn of the agricultural year.
>
> (Exod. 34:22 CSB)

> You are to celebrate the LORD's festival on the fifteenth day of the seventh month for seven days after you have gathered the produce of the land.
>
> (Lev. 23:39a CSB)

On this occasion of remembering the distant desert past, God also called His people to remember the *recent* past: the year's harvest, whatever that harvest may have been. He invited them to recount more than only His faithfulness and goodness to their ancestors; he invited them to remember His faithfulness in their personal mountains and valleys and His goodness in their thirsting and quenching. And that is what the Jerusalem worshipers did. Fingers worked with foliage in the shade of breezy booths, fully engaged in remembering God's protection and sustenance, past and present woven together. The feast's combination of booth and lulav endures as a tangible symbol of God's kept promises.

God's assignment of two different names and purposes for this pilgrimage feast—Booths and Ingathering—is another reason why people began referring to it simply as "the Feast," *HaGag*.[56] The simplified name captures that combination of past and present, God's faithfulness to our ancestors and to us. Whether the past year brought abundance or famine—literally or figuratively—God carried the Israelites, the pilgrims, and us to *this* season. That is why the words of the *Shehecheyanu* roll off our tongues, out of the wellspring of our hearts, during so many occasions in Judaism. Literally meaning "that we are alive," the *Shehecheyanu* is a blessing that expresses gratefulness, faith, and trust:*

> Blessed are You, L-rd our G-d, King of the Universe, who has granted us life, sustained us and enabled us to reach this occasion.**

We offer up this blessing in thanks for something new or special, whether big or small, voicing our wonder and appreciation for a moment. In chanting the *Shehecheyanu*, we recognize that whatever we're experiencing is a gift of God's grace.

As families shared their first meal inside their freshly assembled booths, chanted *Shehecheyanus* drifted over the Jerusalem hillside. The pilgrims' layered refrain feels to me like a prelude to the official worship. When everyone eventually emerged for the first service at the Temple, the pilgrims flooded the streets with their countless bouquets of green and pops of

*This blessing is recited during festivals and special moments to acknowledge and express thanksgiving to God.

**In many Jewish translations and writings, the letter "o" is omitted. This practice developed because God's name is never to be erased or destroyed, and so His titles even in English are not fully spelled out so there is no risk that that will happen. Not all Jewish traditions observe this practice, however.

yellow. God's people moved toward the bronze altar like a rustling field of faithfulness.

Finally reaching the sanctuary courtyard, the worshipers listened to a priest read Psalm 118 aloud.[57] As he read the first verse, the people shook their handfuls of bounty and beauty in unison, in a fluid succession of waves in all directions:[58] "Oh give thanks to the LORD, for he is good; for his steadfast love endures forever!" Lulavs waved up and down, then circled east, south, west, and north. As he called out verse 25, they waved again: "LORD, save us! Hosanna!"* Up, down, circle around. And then the final verse of the worship psalm: "Give thanks to the LORD, for he is good; his love endures forever." Up, down, and all around. *Amen*.

The people's response to the psalmist's words were essentially a liturgy of movement, wordless worship to the God of creation. The nation's adoration swept through the autumn air. Branches waved in confession that all the crops—and the sun and rain that made them possible—came from the divine Provider. Green and yellow swirled over the mountain in a dance proclaiming that God's presence is everywhere, sustaining everyone. Leaves rustled in proclamation that His dominion extends over the whole earth, stretching to the heights of heaven and reaching to the depths below. It is *all* His.

Those hundreds of thousands of lulavs waving in synchrony on Mount Zion's hillside must have been a breathtaking sight to behold. The literal bundles of joy rippled through the Temple complex, raised by every image bearer strong enough to lift this tangible hallelujah.[59] Whether with the new strength of children or the fading strength of elders, *this* act was the great celebration of the feast. Not the booths, not the larger-than-life lampstands. It is in waving the lulav that we respond to Adonai. It is in waving the lulav that we proclaim and rejoice in the

*Hosanna is Hebrew for "save, please" or "save us, we pray."

faithfulness of our King. In time, this instrument of worship became not only the universal symbol of the Feast of Booths but a symbol of Israel itself. It is the branch and bough, the frond and fruit, that are stamped on ancient coins and carved in Jewish catacombs.[60]

Over time, waving the biblical branches and fruit grew into something more. Yes, the nation continued to wave them in an act of beautifully synchronized worship, but the lulav also blossomed into something personal. It became a full-bodied pledge. Each piece of the bundled bounty became symbolic of the worshipers themselves, of ourselves. The tall, unbending palm frond represents our backbone. It calls us to stand for God's truth, justice, and goodness in all our dealings. The eye-shaped myrtle leaves remind us to fix our vision on the Eternal One. The lip-shaped willow leaves inspire us to honor God with speech that is wise, self-controlled, and kind. Finally, the heart-shaped *etrog*, the fruit of bounty held in our left hand, represents the heart beating in the left side of our chest. It reminds us that our hearts are made and known intimately by our Creator. My own heart warms every time I hold that yellow citrus in my hand. When I feel its weight and smell its aroma each autumn, I rest in the reassurance that God knows my dreams and my fears, my joys and my griefs.

Every time we carry this symbolic foliage in our arms, we cradle a beautiful reminder that we, too, are completely and altogether God's. Shaking the lulav up and down and all around as a congregation, we not only give thanks for God's bounty but give thanks for our individual lives as well. We offer up our whole selves to the sovereign and steadfast love of God. Waving the lulav is synchronized worship and synchronized submission. It is a personal and public recommitment to love the Lord our God with all that we are and with all that we have, to stand and watch and speak and long for God.

Even now, dispersed around the globe, the children of Adonai still offer our thanksgiving through these bouquets, waved both in community and inside our personal booths. But back in the days of the Temple, when the pilgrims walked and worshiped atop Mount Zion, Jerusalem must have looked like a lush field ripe with bounty, billowing with the movement of God's people. At the end of each feast day, that field grew even more lush and dense as the pilgrims ascended the Temple Mount one last time. Each person received a single willow—still fresh from the nearby village of Motza.[61] The graceful branches passed from the full arms of Levites into the expectant hands of worshipers. And then, in wave after wave, the pilgrims approached the bronze altar and circled it, their single willow in one hand and their lulav still in the other.[62] This ritual was the one occasion all year that brought non-Levites this close to Adonai's altar, that massive thirty-four-foot square of bronze that towered seventeen feet high (2 Chron. 4:1).[63] Hearts must have pounded at this rare proximity to the place of sacrifice.[64]

Circling the altar, each person gently propped their willow against it so that the top of each bough bent and swayed overhead toward the center. Willows, the weakest twig of the lulav—fragile and without fragrance or taste—alone adorned the place of redemption each day.[65] With each willow, God's people slowly constructed a verdant shelter around the altar. It echoed the shelters they had built for themselves on the hillside, which themselves were an echo of the booths their ancestors had built in the wilderness. It was a beautiful picture of the Redeemer's sheltering presence during those forty years of sojourn, and it was also a gentle reminder of the way He offered to renew them, over and over, through that place of sacrifice. As the willow booth took shape each evening, the people processed behind the priest, singing out, "Save us, we beseech thee, O Lord!" (Ps. 118:25a RSV). Punctuating the people's hosannas came the piercing cry of the ram's horn, that ancient reminder of humanity's very first substitute on the altar: the ram caught in the thicket, offered up in the place of Isaac on that very same mountain.

So many times, Jesus had placed a willow at that altar right alongside His family and friends. Each year, the nation's hosannas enveloped Him. Each year, their countless cries for salvation filled the ears of the One who had come to bring it. The piercing ram's horn would remind Jesus—as if He could forget—of His own substitution for them—and for us—on the altar. The Messiah's self-control, His single-minded focus on mission over moment, was nothing short of otherworldly, especially during His last year. This willow ritual—and all the hosannas that punctuated it—must have gripped Jesus with the inescapable reality of the coming cross, only six months away.

I wonder if a building wave of trepidation, a foretaste of Gethsemane, swept through Jesus with every willow He blessed and placed that week, knowing that at the next pilgrimage feast, He would place Himself on the altar of the cross. Jesus would soon become the better willow: the Redeemer who grew up as a tender shoot without anything to draw people to Him, but who would soon adorn the altar in ways no one could imagine (Isa. 11:1; 53:2).

In the spring, Jesus—*the* Branch—would become the ultimate sheltering sacrifice, the answer to all the hosannas of all time (Isa. 4:2; 11:1; Jer. 23:5). His temporary shelter of flesh would finally meet its end on a very different altar: an altar not adorned by the loveliness of lush willows but one that would leave the Son of God exposed on a splintering crossbeam of wood. He would be deprived even of the sheltering embrace of the Father. Yet for the joy set before Him—our forever presence with Him—Jesus chose to endure the unthinkable. And so, as family and friends and strangers and enemies cried out for salvation, Jesus, too, placed His willows and waved His lulav. He offered up His own heart and eyes, lips and spine—His everything—to the Father's will.

If those moments with the willows and hosannas around the altar threatened to engulf the Son of Man in darkness, the colossal torches in the Temple courtyard quickly would have reminded Him what it was all for. Roaring to life in those twilight moments, the flames bathed Jesus in light each night, transforming God's mountain into a brilliant beacon. That ritual was another symbol of what the Messiah was meant to do: to destroy darkness altogether. The sixteen larger-than-life lamps illuminating Mount Zion were an advance celebration. It was Israel's way of rejoicing in the promise of God's light. The sky-high flares that illuminated the entire city were an expression of their complete trust in a promise God had spoken through Zechariah, a promise that would come to fruition on the Feast of Booths one day. This promise was read by the nation on the first day of the feast, every single year—and still is.

> On that day the sources of light will no longer shine, yet there will be continuous day! Only the LORD knows how this could happen. There will be no normal day and night, for at evening time it will still be light. In the end, the enemies of Jerusalem who survive the plague will go up to Jerusalem each year to worship the King, the LORD of Heaven's Armies, and to celebrate the Festival of Shelters.
>
> (Zech. 14:6–7, 16 NLT)

This is what led the nation to rejoice with all their might on the mountain each night. *This* is why the great Gamaliel juggled fire and lifted himself from prostrating in the dirt to thumbstands in the air. God's people obliterated the night on top of Jerusalem to celebrate the joy yet to come. They lit those massive flares to hasten the day when divine light, instead of burning oil, would illuminate the dark, to hasten the day when the Messiah's magnificent arrival would draw the eyes of every nation to this mountain and all peoples of the world would answer Jerusalem's call (Isa. 60:1–3). The greater beacon would not only illuminate the holy hilltop, but bring light and life to the whole wide weary world. *That* is what the sky-high torches were ultimately about.

After the feast ended and the flames went dark, their brilliance remained seared in everyone's minds. Even extinguished, the golden lampstands towered overhead, providing shade as the people dismantled their booths. The people reminisced about the light and joy they had shared. It was in the midst of the deconstruction, reminiscing, and hoping that the young rabbi from Galilee stood in the Temple courts and cleared His throat. With one simple pronouncement, Jesus harnessed the people's memories of the blazing flares that had pushed back the darkness every night of the feast. He tapped into their remembrances of the fiery pillar in the wilderness and their longing for the coming Messiah's eternal light. Jesus wrapped the past, present, and future around Himself and offered a gift that no one was expecting that day: "I am the light of the world," Jesus declared. "Anyone who follows me will never walk in the darkness but will have the light of life" (John 8:12 CSB).

Jesus's words were not mere metaphor. They were not simply a parable about light and darkness. Every faithful Jew in Jerusalem knew that God is, Himself, light—which meant that they knew Jesus was not simply saying, in a very poetic way, that His teaching would light their way. Jesus's claim to be the Light of the World was not about what He *does* but about who He *is*. Jesus was proclaiming, in unmistakable Jewish language, that He is God, the Eternal One clothed in light (Ps. 104:2). And in that shocking declaration, Jesus not only asserted His authority to offer the light of life, but He promised to share it with anyone who followed Him. *Anyone*.

The days of Zechariah's prophecy were now upon them, dawning over all the nations. The Messiah was preparing the way for ultimate, eternal rejoicing. He was about to kindle the light of eternity for all humanity, inviting anyone and everyone to a place where darkness would be extinguished for good. The pilgrims surely could not help but have pondered these things when they took their leave of Jesus and the Temple Mount.

Making their way toward the city gates, families bid farewell to Jerusalem in the traditional way after the Feast of Booths, twice calling out, "O altar, beauty is to you!"[66] There is no question that the altar would be beautiful when the pilgrims returned to Jerusalem for Passover in the spring. Except it would be beautiful and terrible all at once. And it would give way to eternal shelter, wholeness, and light for us all.

Eternal shelter, wholeness, and light. Booths, branches, and flames. They are pictures of things I never fully understood when I was young. They are pictures of a *person* I had never imagined when I was young. Yet there Jesus was, in my beloved Jerusalem, promising light and life as only God can. There He stood, throwing open the doors to a place where darkness would be drowned in light forever. My pilgrim ancestors stood dumbfounded that day. And while some believed and others protested, they all carried His words back home, turning them over and over.

I remember turning God's shocking words over and over in my own mind during that silent drive home so many years ago in Virginia. And I remember believing them. Jesus had, astonishingly, become my light, my shelter, and my sacrifice. I recognized Him, with a suddenness that took my breath away, as the Messiah—the One before whom I will forever wave my offerings of praise, thanksgiving, and joy. The Feast of Booths stretches toward an eternity of magnificent celebration, of never-ending beauty and bounty. And it comes with a hand-delivered invitation to all humanity, to dwell there with grateful hearts, forever looking toward the Light lifted up.

Jerusalem calls us to rejoice.

CHAPTER 6

Greatest Day

> O Israel, wait for the LORD; for with the LORD is steadfast love and great power to redeem.
>
> Psalm 130:7 Tanakh Translation

I am claustrophobic. Cramped spaces cause me so much panic that, during my second pilgrimage—the one when I was a brand-new believer carrying a contraband New Testament in my suitcase—I steadfastly refused to descend into the caverns underneath the Wailing Wall.* Despite my urge to see the ancient treasures in that sacred space, and regardless of my cousins' jesting and my elders' urging, I would not set foot inside that dark tunnel. Instead, I peered inside and turned on my heel, exchanging wonder for fear.

Twenty-eight years later, visiting the Holy Land with my own little family, I did not make the same mistake. On a gorgeous

*Also known as the Western Wall, it is all that remains of the retaining wall that surrounded the Temple Mount. People gather there for worship and prayer, and it is the wall in which many people wedge written prayers in the cracks between the massive hewn stones.

summer morning—the Fourth of July, to be exact—my husband, two children, and I left the breezy courtyard oasis of the Christ Church guesthouse and made our way down Mount Zion to the City of David National Park. Waiting for our assigned entry time, my husband, David, and I strolled to the overlook and admired the panoramic view of small homes stacked side by side on the hillside. I quickly fell in love with this view of Jerusalem, one I had never seen before. Our teenage daughter, meanwhile, was busy falling in love with a steady stream of stray cats that came to curl up beside her on a shaded bench. Hearing our number called from the window, the five of us donned our water shoes and prepared to descend into the rock beneath Jerusalem, into the darkness of King Hezekiah's tunnel.

The ancient aqueduct is an absolute marvel of engineering. The fact that people living at the beginning of the Iron Age defied gravity and guided water uphill without pumps or machinery, deep within the core of the mountain, astounds me. In fact, the tunnel was so well engineered in 701 BC that water *still* flows uphill from the Gihon Spring on the outskirts of the city up into Mount Zion today. The spring is a lesson in physics, too. *Gihon* literally means "gushing," and that is exactly what it does. The spring intermittently gushes out of an underground cave shaped like a giant watering can. The water level in the cave must rise to the point of reaching the end of the spout before any water will flow out. When the groundwater finally does fill the cave to the tip of this siphon, which people say is the diameter of a coin, the spring surges suddenly, emptying the underground reservoir and leaving the spring quiet until the water level rises again.[67]

This unique spring is what made Jerusalem inhabitable in the first place, long before Hezekiah, King David, or even Abraham's descendants arrived on the scene. As the only reliable source of fresh water in the area, the Gihon Spring provided a way to irrigate the fields in the Kidron Valley. This water source meant more than only agricultural flourishing for God's covenant people, though. The Gihon also provided the naturally flowing water—*mayim chay'yim*—necessary for purification from many kinds of uncleanness, including the uncleanness of death.* It is beautifully poetic, I think, that one of Jerusalem's ancient nicknames is "Navel of the Earth," since it is watered physically and spiritually by a spring that gushes from inside its "belly."[68]

I allowed my fascination with the Gihon Spring to wash away my anxiety as we followed my father-in-law below the ground. The five of us shuffled and splashed through the darkness of Hezekiah's ancient tunnel, feeling our way through tight spaces and jagged turns. At one point we encountered a replica of ancient Hebrew writing that had been carved into the tunnel wall just after its completion. The original inscription described the breakneck efforts of two separate work crews simultaneously carving out the channel.[69] With one starting from inside the city wall and the other from the valley below, the crews raced to finish diverting Jerusalem's water supply into the city before Assyria's impending attack (2 Chron. 32:30; 2 Kings 20:20).[70] The two groups made their way toward one another, hammering and chipping furiously through the dolomite and limestone. Somehow, without modern communication or ultrasound, they worked to within just a few meters of one another. Suddenly hearing the strike of each other's pickaxes through the solid rock, the euphoric laborers quickly created a sharp turn to connect their two tunnels. Now, thousands of years later, I was walking through that very same jagged turn.

My family continued making our way up the channel, our feet splashing through the icy water while our hands grazed the pick marks from that hasty excavation. My father-in-law—a retired

***Mayim chay'yim* is typically translated in English as "fresh water," "flowing water," or "running water." For examples, see Genesis 26:19; Leviticus 14; and Numbers 19:16–17.

Marine fighter pilot and longtime Boy Scout leader who's spent plenty of time in dark, cramped spaces—marveled at how difficult this work must have been. Engulfed by heat, fatigue, and the din of metal on stone, the workers had toiled even as their torches consumed precious oxygen. Honestly, it wasn't hard for us to imagine it, because the tunnel is still as rough cut, jagged, and dark as it was nearly three millennia ago. Every so often, a dingy light bulb would light up a bit of my son's red T-shirt a few yards ahead. He was like an underground flare, reassuring me that I hadn't been left behind.

For forty-five minutes, we made our way together through the channel, sometimes crouching, sometimes walking sideways, sometimes wading through water up to our knees. Then, abruptly, we stepped into the soft breeze and brilliant sun of midday Jerusalem. As my eyes slowly adjusted, I turned and saw the stream—the one that had been rushing uphill over our shuffling feet—now emptying right beside us into the Pool of Siloam.[71]

Yes. *That* Pool of Siloam. For seven hundred years before Jesus took His first breath of earth's air, the Pool of Siloam had been filling up with water from the Gihon Spring, delivered directly from Hezekiah's tunnel. Thanks to the skilled work of Hezekiah's team, not only was Jerusalem's water source protected from outside enemies, but God's people could now also receive cleansing without venturing down the hillside, outside the city walls. Instead, Hezekiah's tunnel carried that *mayim chay'yim*—living, flowing water—up Jerusalem's hill. Bubbling up near the sanctuary, Gihon's fresh water offered cleansing right where people gathered for worship and ministry.

Siloam's sacred waters also began rippling their way somewhere else: into the most joyous celebration of the Jewish year, the Feast of Booths. Sometime during the glory days of Solomon's Temple, in the years before the exile to Babylon, Israel added a water ritual to the Feast of Booths. The people were keenly aware of water's power, especially as they waved their bundled branches each morning and thanked God for the bounty of the land. Whether abundant or meager, the pilgrims' storehouses back home testified to the importance of water.

By the time everyone arrived at the feast, Israel's fields were dry and full of stubble, awaiting the quench of winter's rain to prepare the soil for spring's seed. According to tradition handed down from Moses, the amount of rainfall for each year is determined by God during the Feast of Booths.[72] So Israel created a water ceremony, adding it to the week's worship. Each day of the feast, God's people expressed gratitude for the bounty He had just provided and asked Him to send rain in the year ahead. Just as with the waving lulavs, the water ritual was a coupling together of giving thanks for the past and expressing dependence for the future.

Israel named the water ritual *Simchat Beit Ha'Shoavah*: Rejoicing at the Place of the Water Drawing. The place of this water drawing was none other than the Pool of Siloam, that sacred pool filled by Hezekiah's aqueduct. The daily worship at those healing waters was more than a straightforward, agricultural prayer for rain. It was a boisterous parade, a community celebration, and a concert of praise. This exuberant ritual clearly meant more to Israel than simply petitioning God to water their crops. It was about God Himself, who likened His care of Israel to those gently flowing waters of Siloam and who called Himself Israel's source of living, purifying water (Isa. 8:5–6; Jer. 2:13; 17:13).[73] That is why Siloam's pool is considered so incredibly sacred.

Years later, after Nebuchadnezzar's destruction of Jerusalem and the exile in Babylon, Israel made her way back home to those sacred waters. In those years after the remnant returned, God spoke through the prophet Zechariah about the Feast of Booths and the coming Messiah. He spoke not only of never-ending light but also of flowing water. The water ritual swelled with anticipation of that promised future day.

> On that day, He will set His feet on the Mount of Olives, near Jerusalem on the east; and the Mount of Olives shall split across from east to west, and one part of the Mount shall shift to the north and the other to the south, a huge gorge. . . . In that day, there shall be neither sunlight nor cold moonlight, but there shall be a continuous day—only the LORD knows when—of neither day nor night, and there shall be light at eventide. In that day, fresh water shall flow from Jerusalem, part of it to the Eastern Sea and part to the Western Sea, throughout the summer and winter. And the LORD shall be king over all the earth; in that day there shall be one LORD with one name. . . . All who survive of all those nations that came up against Jerusalem shall make a pilgrimage year by year to bow low to the King LORD of Hosts and to observe the Feast of Booths.
>
> (Zech. 14:4, 6–9, 16 JPS85)

Zechariah's prophecy, always read on the first day of the Feast of Booths, foretells not only never-ending daylight but also a never-ending flow of water from Jerusalem's hill. It is a flow that will be unleashed upon the arrival of the Messiah atop that most holy mountain. And so the meaning of the water ritual grew deeper than it had been before the exile. Israel pleaded every day at the sacred pool for rain and for rescue. They pleaded for the near future and the far future, and they hoped that the gap between the two was closing fast. This joy-filled ritual at Siloam's gentle waters expressed Israel's deep, collective longing for the arrival of the Messiah—an arrival that would be marked by the flow of water from Jerusalem, watering the whole world.[74]

Each morning during the Feast of Booths, as the sun rose, the rooster crowed, and the colossal lampstands went dark, the pilgrims expectantly held their breath for the sound of silver trumpets blown by two priests at the Temple's Upper Gate.[75] The three unmistakable blasts signaled that the water-fetching priest had reached the tenth of the fifteen courtyard steps.[76] The trumpet blasts were also the people's invitation to join him on his walk to Siloam's sacred waters.[77] Those clarion calls were beautiful music to everyone's ears, because they beckoned every non-Levite to become part of the most joyous worship ritual of the year.[78] The pilgrims may have served as unofficial worship leaders along the pilgrimage roads, but in these moments on Jerusalem's hill, all of God's people were folded into the priestly choir and welcomed into the joy-filled beckoning of the Messiah. It is not an exaggeration to say that the water drawing ritual at the Pool of Siloam was a national treasure.

Emerging from their makeshift booths at the trumpets' call, the pilgrims excitedly formed a procession behind the water fetcher, accompanying him down the hillside with waves of jubilant song. What a glorious vision: the people of God unified in hope and in song, together drawing near to His sacred waters. It was made all the more beautiful by the lush backdrop of the King's Garden, with its terraces of blooms spilling down into the valley below, fed by the same gushing spring.[79]

With so many bright eyes upon him in those moments, the priest knelt to the pool and filled a small golden flask with Siloam's waters. Rising with the precious cache in his hands, the priest turned and began his ascent back to the Temple Mount. Accompanying him all the way back to the courtyard, the throng of worshipers continued singing praises to the God who faithfully cared for them like Siloam's gentle, refreshing waters. As the procession passed through the Water Gate (so named because of this very ritual), trumpets greeted them and the treasure they brought.[80]

Reaching the foot of the altar, the water fetcher joined another priest who held a similar flask. This priest's vessel was filled not with water but with the day's wine offering. Together, the pair ascended the ramp to the top of the altar just as the morning sacrifice was placed on the grate.[81] With reverent precision, the water-bearer stepped to the west and the wine-bearer to the east, and both began to pour. The offerings of water and wine flowed from each priest's golden flask into a silver basin resting at his feet on top of the altar.[82] Even as the offerings were pouring into the vessels, they immediately began to drain through a perforated spout at the bottom of each one. In perfect synchrony, the basins ran dry at precisely the same moment, their differently sized spouts engineered specifically to account for the different viscosity of water and wine.[83]

The pilgrims waved their festal foliage up and down and all around, toward heaven above, the earth below, and the far reaches of the whole world. All the while, the Levites sang, the flutes trilled, and the wine and water flowed. This moment is, in fact, precisely where the last chapter brought us: Jerusalem's hillside looking like a billowing field of green and gold as the nation swayed in worship, circling the altar and leaving their willows. This is the moment each day when praises and pleas flowed from the people's lips as they gathered around the altar—still wet with water and wine—anticipating God's rescue together. Hosanna![84]

On the very last day of the feast, though, the ritual reached a fever pitch. In fact, rabbis used to say that anyone who hadn't experienced the water ritual on that last day of the Feast of Booths had never experienced true joy.[85] On that last and greatest day, the procession to the Pool of Siloam swelled in number and volume. That morning, more priests and Levites joined in, blowing trumpets. Vocalists left the courtyard to lead the people in hymns all the way down to the sacred pool. All of the worshipers rejoiced together through songs and prayers anchored in the hope of Zechariah's prophecy. And they rejoiced in the hope proclaimed through the Scripture read during the water festival on that last and greatest day:

> With joy you will draw water from the wells of
> salvation.
>
> (Isa. 12:3 NIV)

The priest may have been drawing water from the Pool of Siloam that day, but the people knew that greater waters were coming. The sky-high lampstands, the juggling of torches, and all the acrobatics were only glimpses of the greater joy to come. Their future joy would be marked not only by never-ending light and living water flowing down Jerusalem's mountain but also by God's Spirit saturating them from the inside out.[86] That is what the feast's seventh-day Scripture about the wells of salvation was all about: not only literal water flowing from Jerusalem's mountain but also the Holy Spirit streaming from heaven.[87]

Celebrating that future assurance, the procession made its way back to the Temple Mount. But this time, the worshipers didn't circle the altar just once. On that last and greatest day, they circled it seven times. They also did something altogether different with their branches. Walking around the place of sacrifice, God's people cast down palm fronds and beat willow branches around the altar until the leaves fell off and the fronds were in pieces.[88] It was nicknamed, in fact, the "Day of Beating Branches."

This seventh-day practice, which went back to the time of the prophets, was a jolting shift from the verdant willow shelter they had built around the altar on the other days of the feast.[89] It makes me wonder what Jesus thought about all of it. What went through His mind each morning when the water and wine flowed onto the altar, next to the bound sacrifice? Did He think about the water and blood that would soon flow from

His side? Did His stomach churn when everyone dashed their branches on the ground with the intensity of their messianic longing? Did His heart quicken during the extended prayer for rain on that *Hoshanaha Rabbah*, the last and greatest day, at the moment they prayed for the flow of God's abundant water? We can't pretend to know what Jesus thought or felt in those moments, but we do know what He said. We know, because the disciple John shared with us his own sermon notes from that day. It was a two-sentence message, preached against the backdrop of the booths, the branches, and the sacred waters flowing uphill from the belly of the mountain.

It was that particular sermon that I thought about when I finally stood atop the sprawling Temple Mount for the first time. I remember breathing deeply with eyes closed, envisioning the gleaming white Temple of Elohim as it had been on that first-century day. I pictured the sanctuary rising from the massive plateau where we stood—thirty-seven acres of dressed limestone crowning the top of Mount Zion. I visualized the courtyard swelling with a multitude of worshipers, young and old, still cradling their branches. I could see them weaving their way through the press of people, everyone searching out different rabbis who were preparing to teach, and situating themselves on the ground for a final festival lesson. Assembling in clusters throughout the Temple complex was the only possible way to hear a sermon in such an expansive place in those ancient days.

Rabbi Jesus was one of the many teachers preparing to teach in the Temple complex that morning. And on that last and greatest day, there were things He wanted people to hear. There were promises He wanted ringing in the pilgrims' ears as they journeyed back home. There were messages He wanted them to share in their communities and ponder before coming back to Jerusalem in the spring for Passover. *The* Passover. The *Passion Week* Passover. So if the dashing of fronds and branches happened to unnerve Him that seventh morning, if the seven laps around the bloodstained altar threatened to overwhelm him, Jesus must have channeled every bit of it into urgency. He stood to teach about that morning's text, about the wells of salvation, just like all the other rabbis who taught in the court that day—except, not at *all* like them.

> Now on the last day of the feast—the great *day*—Jesus stood and cried out, saying,
> "If anyone is thirsty, let him come to me, and let him drink, the one who believes in me.
> Just as the scripture said, 'Out of his belly will flow rivers of living water.'"
>
> (John 7:37–38 LEB)

Earlier in the morning of that last and greatest day, Israel had gathered at Siloam's sacred waters and celebrated God's promise through Isaiah. The words had moved their hearts toward the joy of being quenched and cleansed and restored by the very Spirit of God. The prophecy stirred their yearning to drink salvation from the inexhaustible well of living water, God Himself.

And now, here was rabbi Jesus, rising to His feet in the most public of places on the most crowded of days. In two short sentences, He wove together every Scripture, every song, every wave of branches and every flow of water during the entire Feast of Booths. He could not have been more strategic in His timing or more intentional in His message. With this declaration on the last and greatest day, Jesus answered every single hosanna lifted up by my ancestors that week, proclaiming to everyone within echoing earshot that He was the answer to their prayers, their longing, and their thirst. Jesus let them all know that He was the source of living water who had come to save, heal, and fill.

There Jesus stood, glory in the flesh, with His feet planted on top of Jerusalem's mountain, offering the very thing they had been begging for. In fact, the Hebrew word for salvation found in Isaiah's text that very morning—the one they had all been celebrating—is *yeshua*. The very same word as Jesus's name in Hebrew.

> Therefore with joy you shall draw water out of the wells of *yeshu'ah*.
>
> (Isa. 12:3 HNV)

All week, God's people cried out for God to save them: Hosanna! And now Jesus—*Yeshua*, "salvation"—was here, answering Israel's cries.* Standing among them with Siloam's waters rippling below, Jesus declared that anyone who believed in Him would be filled with the living water of salvation. It was the water they had all been waiting for, and He promised that it soon would bubble up and overflow from inside them. Instead of physical water gushing from inside the belly of the mountain, the Spirit of God would come gushing—*gihon*—from within the innermost parts of *themselves*. Salvation's water had arrived to quench their souls and water the world.

With every word, Jesus was proclaiming in deeply Jewish ways that He was God. Every single pilgrim knew it. Every single Levite knew it, all five hundred who served at the feast.[90] Every single priest knew it, all twenty-four teams of them.[91] Even the temple guards were mesmerized (John 7:45–47). Startlingly, Nicodemus the Pharisee began speaking up in Jesus's defense, even to the temple leadership (John 7:50–52). Strong reactions surged through the sea of pilgrims. There was marveling and murmuring, wonder and warning, hope and hostility. They all grasped at Jesus's words, some as an anchor for their thirsty souls, others as a weapon

*The early spelling was Yehoshua, but in later books of Scripture, the name Joshua (the English equivalent) was shorted to Yeshua. Both mean "God saves" and are derived from the same Hebrew root as hosanna: *yāša*, "to save or deliver."

to wield against Him. Debate raged and fractured across the Temple complex.

When I try to wrap my head around this scene, I often think back to that summer day in Virginia when God spoke to me in the middle of a very different crowd of worshipers. I remember feeling a surge of unbridled joy mixed with fear, like a yearning to run headlong toward cool water while also fearing that the whole thing was a mirage. I imagine that, in some ways, the last and greatest day felt something like that for the pilgrims who recognized their thirst and wanted to believe the One who was offering never-ending water.

Whether overtaken by hope or doubt or anger, each pilgrim would continue to ponder Jesus's words throughout that day, replaying the scene in their minds as they broke camp and packed up their belongings. They would mull over His declarations about water and light while allowing the children to finally sink their teeth into the golden fruit they had been clutching each day.[92] They would discuss and debate His words along the dusty roads home, parched and thinking about water.

For the pilgrims taking the northern route, toward places like Sidon and Tyre, there was one area they would take care to avoid, no matter how parched they became: Samaria. Samaritans were a people group who adopted some aspects of Judaism but did not learn or follow the Jewish Scriptures.[93] At times they supported Israel but at other times came against them.[94] As a result, during Jesus's day, the two didn't associate or think well of each other at all (Luke 10:30–37; John 4:9). This is why Jesus's parable of the good Samaritan was so striking (Luke 10).

But if the pilgrims had chosen to stop in the Samaritan village of Sychar that year, if they had opted to draw water from Jacob's well near the field he had given to his favored son, Joseph, they would have been astonished. Because there they would have found a community already placing their hope in Jesus's promise of living water (John 4:5, 39–42). A community of people they never would have expected. The pilgrims would have learned that Jesus had already made this audacious promise to someone else. Not in the most public of places, like the Temple courts, but in the most lonely of spots—a noonday well:

> Jesus replied, "If you only knew the gift God has for you and who you are speaking to, you would ask me, and I would give you living water. . . . Those who drink the water I give will never be thirsty again. It becomes a fresh, bubbling spring within them, giving them eternal life." . . . Then Jesus told her, "I AM the Messiah!"
>
> (John 4:10, 14, 26 NLT)

The Samaritan woman was an outcast woman in an outcast land. Yet there, on the outskirts of the covenant and of her own community, underneath the noonday sun, she received Jesus's personal offer of living water. She, thirsty for water from both the well of Jacob and the well of salvation, accepted the joy of Yeshua's cup. Refreshed and revived, the woman simply could not contain herself. Running back to the village, she shared about Jesus with the very people that she, in her shame, had been avoiding by going to the well in the heat of the day. She told them everything, and they all came running. They, too, were thirsty—for all the reasons that broken people thirst. And at their insistence, Jesus remained with them for two days, teaching and encouraging them with the good news of living water.

Zechariah's promised flood to the nations was beginning to trickle down Jerusalem's hill. It was being passed around by thirsty Samaritans and carried home by covenant pilgrims. Picturing these first cascades makes me think about the Gihon Spring, with its cave of slowly accumulating water. The groundwater rising inside that cave, then at long last reaching the spout and gushing out, is a powerful visual of what was soon to happen in Jerusalem. God's living water would soon reach its tipping point as well. And when it finally overflowed, the sacred waters would not stream uphill through Hezekiah's tunnel. Nor would they be confined to Siloam's pool. Instead, living water—the Holy Spirit of God (John 7:38–39)—would pour throughout the entire earth, reviving every thirsty soul asking to be filled.

Jerusalem calls us to drink.

CHAPTER 7

Grandma's Table

> Were it not for the Lord, who was on our side, let Israel now declare; were it not for the Lord, who was on our side when men assailed us . . . the waters would have carried us off, the torrent would have swept over us; over us would have swept the seething waters. . . . Our help is the name of the Lord, maker of heaven and earth.
>
> Psalm 124:1–2, 4–5, 9 JPS85

Scooping my toddler up from her obstacle course of busy feet and yippy dogs, I caught a glimpse of my youngest sister walking toward my husband. Even though they stood just a few feet from me, I couldn't hear a single word passing between them—not over the din of scraping chairs, clanking silverware, seven raucous children, and no fewer than five Jewish mothers spanning three generations. Instructions and quips sailed across the tables cobbled together in my grandparents' sunroom. The most authoritative voice belonged, of course, to my Grandma Arliene. Her lilting Brooklyn timbre soared above us all, directing the placement of matzah, horseradish, and saucers of salt water.

We weren't in Brooklyn anymore, though. We were gathered in their new Florida home. And by this time, my grandma was known as Grandma Bell, having been rebranded by the great-grandkids on account of the round earth pendant that she wore around her neck at all times. The little planet mesmerized them with its tiny bell singing inside like a soft Japanese chime. It seemed that—intentionally or not—Grandma had come up with her own kind of Mr. Flugel-Flaggle: something that drew the little ones onto her lap like a magnet. There they would snuggle and tap the golden globe with uncharacteristic gentleness. Their delight never failed to evoke a steady stream of coos from my grandma, as well as that marvelous, carefree, teenage laugh of hers. No one loved life like Grandma Arliene. No one loved life like *either* of my grandmas. Arliene's and Marion's eyes seemed to twinkle mischievously all the time, like they had a fantastical secret they were just on the verge of divulging. And they both seemed to fill the air with music, whether singing or humming, playing, or laughing.

But the Passover table of my youth belonged primarily to Arliene. And now, as I hoisted my daughter to my waist, Grandma Arliene was neither singing nor laughing. Instead, hands on hips, she feigned exasperation while telling each of us what to do and exactly how to do it. The truth is that she wasn't really exasperated. It was all a ruse. Arliene could not have been happier to see all her chicks chattering away, finally gathered together after "much too long a time!" It *had* been too long a time—more than a decade since we had all shared a table. The years since my decision to follow Jesus had been fraught with hurt and misunderstanding and tiptoeing around. We had all tried to lean in as best we knew how, making plenty of missteps along the way, including me. By this time, though, most of us had visited together here and there, gathered in small numbers or in large numbers at one cousin's bat mitzvah and another's wedding. But we hadn't all come together at *this* table.

Now, at long last, after our ten years of marriage and the addition of our two children, my husband finally found himself at my grandparents' treasured Passover table. I, at long last, found *myself* at my grandparents' Passover table. It was the first time since Palmyra, seventeen years earlier. All that I had feared was lost was on its way to being found.

My youngest sister recognized the awkwardness in the midst of the Passover mayhem and was stepping into the gap like she has always done. She is the one who, at sixteen years old, persuaded our father that he and his two younger daughters should be part of my church wedding, even though many in his family would not attend, including his parents. "You know she's right," urged my middle sister the next day as she and my father walked in their neighborhood. My father agreed. This turned out to be a significant turning point, and I am forever grateful for my sisters' steadfast love for all of us. A few months later, I would walk down the aisle linking arms with both my stepdad and my father and would stand at the altar with all three sisters by my side. One of my very favorite photos from that day is a candid of me, eyes closed, just before stepping into the sanctuary. I waited there with a dad on each arm, both of them beaming down at me.

Now here I was, a decade later, watching my husband amid the happy turbulence of four generations preparing for a three-hour tour of the exodus. My sister joined him in the middle of the melee. "I'm glad you're here," she had said to David, building her characteristically warm and insightful bridge. "I know it's probably awkward." And my similarly warm and insightful husband—who refused to ever complain about his rough entry into my clan—smiled and told her, with complete sincerity, that he was really happy to be there. And he was. David has loved them all—and they all have loved him—more than I could have possibly imagined back in our early days.

"Actually," he shrugged, "Jesus's Last Supper was a Passover meal, so I'm looking forward to experiencing what that's like." My sister's bright blue eyes—the ones that we all share—widened. From my floor-level vantage point, I could see her eyebrows rise, but I couldn't make out anything said between them. Had someone done something, said something? I feared the worst. It's what I do. But of course everyone was perfectly wonderful. I found out later what the two had been saying to one another, and that the words escaping my sister's lips in that moment were simply, "It was?" She didn't know. *I* hadn't known.

This oblivion to the basics of the gospel would shock most American Christians. In the evangelical circles I've traveled in and through, particularly in the South, most people are genuinely surprised to learn that not everyone in America knows who Jesus is. Most evangelicals I speak with assume that non-Christians in the United States know everything about the life, ministry, and mission of Jesus and have chosen to not believe it. But I had had no idea, not until Palmyra. My father didn't know what I believed, either. Not until I finally worked up the courage to ask him during a wedding planning discussion. When I told him I simply believe that Jesus is the Jewish Messiah, foretold by Moses and the prophets, his eyebrows rose, too. "Really?" was his wary response.

I rarely think about those days now, that sad season of guarded distance, because God brought us through it. Even though no one in my family currently shares my belief in Jesus, God has restored every broken relationship. The warmth between us, especially with my father and my grandparents, grew even deeper as we made our way back to one another. And now, I was once again at my father's parents' Passover table with my sisters and cousins and aunt and uncle. It was the very same crew I had traveled with to the Holy Land the week after meeting Jesus. And we were gathering together just like old times, now with our own children at the table. Together, we prepared to celebrate our great Redeemer—they, by remembering the exodus deliverance, and me, remembering the layered deliverance of both Egypt and Calvary.

Yet we weren't only gathering with one another in my grandparents' sunroom. We were also joining in spirit with loved ones and strangers across the nation and the ocean—including my mom's side of the family, who were scattered between New Jersey, Iowa, and Wisconsin. What is incredible about celebrations like Passover is the awareness that the entire worldwide Jewish diaspora is worshiping with the same words, the same foods, the same songs, and the same Scriptures—all in the exact same order, simply staggered across time zones. The Hebrew word *seder* actually means "order," and it is this ordered worship meal that unifies us in profound ways. The Jerusalem Temple may be buried beneath thousands of years of stone and strife, but Jews continue to pilgrimage together in spirit, celebrating redemption as one nation in united, ancient worship.

> Now this day shall be a reminder for you;
> you are to celebrate it as a pilgrimage-celebration
> for YHWH;
> throughout your generations, as a law for the ages you
> are to celebrate it!
> And it will be, when your children say to you: What
> does this service [mean] to you?
> then say: It is the sacrificial-meal of Passover
> to YHWH,
> who passed over the houses of the Children of Israel in
> Egypt . . .
>
> (Exod. 12:14, 26–27a The Schocken Bible)[95]

God designed the Passover feast to be a Bible lesson shared around the dinner table. It is an occasion to teach the next generation about His mighty rescue out of Egypt. It is a time to marvel at His fierce love and inexhaustible power. Fittingly, the written guide that leads us through the seder worship is titled *Haggadah*—literally, "the retelling." While dads or grandpas usually serve as the master of ceremonies, the rest of the family, including the children, take turns going around and around the table, reading the next remembrance or Scripture from the Haggadah. Of course, this also means the seder can get pretty noisy. But, so was the actual exodus we are commemorating, I imagine!

Many people liken the Haggadah to a script for a play, because it contains not only all the words for us to say and to sing but also very specific instructions for who, when, and how to say them. There is also one key bit of ancient instruction that makes the Haggadah much more than a mere history lesson or script to read through. The Talmud teaches us to recount the exodus as if we ourselves had been personally rescued from Egypt and its yoke of slavery.[96] After all, God's Passover command was that His people were to "remember that *you* were slaves in Egypt and the Lord your God redeemed *you* from there" (Deut. 24:18 NIV, emphasis added).

And so, when we sit at the Passover table, we don't speak of *them* being oppressed or about *their* escape from Egypt, but of *our* oppression and God's deliverance of *us*. We recite as though remembering our own cries of anguish under a yoke too great to bear. We remember as though we were the ones huddled inside, with lamb's blood still wet on the doorframe, as the horror of the Death Angel passed through the land and over us. We remember as though we were among the people caught at the edge of the Red Sea, death swimming before us and closing in behind us. That we felt the rush of wind as God created a path of life into the freedom of the wilderness. We, the rescued, eat and retell our tale about God's deliverance with the amazement and joy of the people who experienced it firsthand.

The symmetry of the seder retelling is exquisite. We share two cups before the dinner break and two cups afterward.[97] We partake of the unleavened bread smack dab in the middle, right before the actual meal, just like it's been done since Temple times.[98] The seder worship is so essential to the Jewish experience that rabbis decreed no one should be deprived of the opportunity to recline at the Passover feast and take all four cups of wine.[99] To be deprived of these things, they said, would be to be deprived of tasting and celebrating God's mighty deliverance. So the entire community was called on to assist families who couldn't afford to prepare a feast or purchase wine for Passover.

Now, you may be asking yourself: *four cups of wine*? Yes, but with a caveat. We drink four cups during the seder as a way of commemorating the four redemption promises that God made on the front end of the exodus rescue (Exod. 6:6–7). But each cup is meant to be small, just shy of a couple ounces, or to be diluted with water in a larger cup. By the end of the evening, the four small cups should amount to a single full cup of wine. Ancient rabbis made it clear that the cups were to be used for remembrance, not impairment.[100] The wine in the four cups paints a picture of both Israel's suffering and God's promises, and it leads us through the remembrance of our journey from oppression to freedom.[101]

> Therefore say to the children of Israel: "I am the LORD;
> **I will bring you out** from under the burdens of the Egyptians,
> **I will rescue you** from their bondage,
> and **I will redeem you** with an outstretched arm and with great judgments.
> **I will take you as My people**, and I will be your God."
> (Exod. 6:6–7 NKJV, emphasis added)

With each cup, we recount God's breathtaking plan of redemption as it unfolded. Using the same wine-stained

Haggadahs year after year, we retell it in the exact same way, with the exact same foods, in the exact same order. We repeat every line, every Scripture, and every song just like we've always done, even though we know exactly how the story plays out. Doing so builds muscle memory in our hearts and minds about the relentless, redemptive love of God.

And it is *wonderful*. Every year, there is a buzz of excitement when we finally settle into our seats. In that opening moment, when Grandpa would rise with the first cup in his hand—whether it was my Grandpa Samuel or Grandpa Jud—the gentle clearing of his throat would call us out of the cacophony of scooting chairs, clanking silverware, and squirmy children. Every head of every age would turn, faces lifted in expectation and affection, as Grandpa drew us into worship of our mighty Redeemer.

We call that first cup *Kadesh*, which means "holy" or "set apart." By launching us into the seder, this first cup lives up to its name by elevating the Passover worship. *Kadesh* represents that first promise of God as He prepared to free the captives, to bring them out from underneath their burdens—to bring *us* out from underneath *our* burdens. I distinctly remember the moment when Grandpa Sandy raised the first cup at that longtime-coming seder in their crowded sunroom. I remember gazing up at him and breathing deep, inhaling the promise of that first cup, and feeling so many burdens fall to the floor as I exhaled. Around the table, each of us raised our own cup to join his, singing the age-old blessing over the fruit of the vine and the One who created it.

And with that, our "ordered" worship began. Don't be fooled, though. Worship at the Passover table may be ordered, but rarely is it order*ly*. There was plenty of fidgeting in that Florida sunroom, just like there was at our seder tables in Brooklyn and Hoboken, in Iowa and Wisconsin—and just like every single seder you may happen to join, in fact. Because, by God's command, the Passover celebration is a family worship service. The only childcare you'll find is someone else's lap down the table!

> They shall eat the meat of the Paschal lamb on that night.
> **They shall eat the meat roasted on fire with Matzoth together with bitter herbs, to remind them of their bitter experiences in Egypt. . . .**
> And when you will come to the land which the Eternal will give you, as He had promised to your fathers, you shall observe this service of the Paschal lamb. **And when your children will say to you: "What is the meaning of this your strange service?" You shall tell them: "This Paschal sacrifice is dedicated to the Eternal . . ."**
>
> (Exod. 12:8, 25–27 Torah Yesharah; emphasis added)

This menu God set for the Passover remembrance—lamb, bitter herbs, and unleavened bread—serves as the prompts in this script recounting the exodus deliverance. Maybe that's where our Jewish proclivity to use foods as a means of remembering all began—like serving latkes (potato pancakes) at Hanukkah to remember the miracle of oil, or baking two braids of challah on Shabbat to recall the double portion of manna in the wilderness. But unlike the culinary symbols we've created on our own, the ritual foods of the seder were curated by God Himself. They help us recall the first Passover, emphasizing the things most important to Him.

When Grandpa Sandy lifted the bitter herbs for us all to see, someone read aloud from their Haggadah about the bitterness of oppression. When he held up a sheet of matzah, someone described the exodus bread, too rushed to rise on the way to freedom. And when Grandpa lifted high the roasted lamb shank, someone recounted how the lamb's blood averted the Angel of Death. Retelling the redemption story together, we taste and see that the Lord is good.

Round and round that table we went, reading, singing, eating, and drinking our way through the exodus narrative for hours. In the midst of all the melodies and remembrances, my eyes met David's across the table time and time again. Honestly, those shared gazes throughout the evening were like an anchor, an Ebenezer in my life. For so long, I felt alone in the company of people that I loved. But I was no longer alone in this. Someone else at the table saw it—saw *Him*—as clearly as I did. Someone else recognized the New in the midst of the Old and marveled at it. From across the table, I watched my beloved husband delighting in the beauty of my beloved Passover, in the midst of my beloved people, recognizing our beloved Messiah in every bit of it, even if no one else did. We saw Jesus in the unleavened bread blessed and broken in my grandfather's hands. We saw Jesus in the "mighty outstretched arm" of rescue glorified over and over in our collective voices. We saw Jesus in the sheltering blood of the sacrificed lambs. I was discovering home in deeper places at that table. Even writing about it now, so many years later, makes me misty.

I wasn't the only misty-eyed one watching my family that evening. As my grandfather led our journey, step by step, through the Passover, I could see my grandmother kvelling (that's Yiddish for being overcome with happiness and pride).* How could she not be? There we were—her children, grandchildren, and great-grandchildren—singing Moses's song from the Red Sea, reading passages from the Torah, and dipping unleavened bread. I remember watching David, leaning over to show our first-grader what to read at his first turn around the table. I can't help but smile when I think about the brand-new little kippah, a gift from my grandma, resting atop his soft

*Yiddish is a hybrid of German, Hebrew, and a little Aramaic. It was spoken predominantly by Jews living in Europe before the Holocaust. My grandparents used to speak it when they didn't want us to know what they were talking about!

hair.** I remember steadying our preschooler as she excitedly rose onto her knees in my lap, one dimpled hand stretching out to dip her parsley in the nearest dish of salt water. The seder salt water is meant to recall our ancestors' desperate tears, but mine were happy tears that night. Because there we all were, living out God's command to teach the next generation about the restoration He brings. And, grace upon grace, our own brokenness was being redeemed at that table of redemption.

When we finally pushed back from the table, the cleanup was quieter and more leisurely than the setup had been. We stretched our legs and returned mismatched chairs to their regular locations. We yawned and collected sterling silver and sippy cups. The older children picked up each Haggadah for safekeeping until next year, the pages stained with a few more drips of salt water and drops of wine than before. Sometimes I wish that we still ended the Passover seder like our ancestors in Jerusalem did, walking out into the night and singing the Hallel psalms (Ps. 113–18) together.*** They are already part of the seder liturgy. But in some communities, people still sing them when departing the meal, just like our ancestors did. On that Passover night in my grandparents' home, I would have loved to sing every one of those repeated *hallelujahs* with my family, sending them up toward the twinkling sky.

Of course, I would love to experience the *whole thing* like the ancient Jerusalem pilgrims did. Because, as frenzied and jubilant as it was in my grandparents' home with twenty-four of us scurrying around, it was only a taste of what Jerusalem felt and sounded and smelled like with upwards of three million people gathered there for Passover.[102] Having traversed those newly smoothed and

**A kippah or yarmulke is a small round head covering, typically worn by men to cover the head during prayer or worship.

***These psalms are called the Hallels, because hallel means "praise" and is the root of "hallelujah." Each of these psalms offers praise to God for rescuing Israel from Egypt.

straightened roads on their way to the spring feast, the exhausted pilgrims couldn't simply collapse on their grandma's sofa or under the crisp linens of a quiet guest room. Instead, their first order of business was to water their equally tired and smelly animals at one of the wells outside the city and then to make their way to the priests ministering to pilgrims as they entered the city.[103] There the travelers would take part in the purification rituals, readying their hearts, minds, and bodies for the worship to come.

Refreshed and purified, the pilgrims' most pressing task was to locate their lodging. Because, unlike the Feast of Booths, when everyone slept outside in their temporary huts, the Passover pilgrims needed to secure accommodations for their stay. For the ones who hadn't made arrangements ahead of time, the search began for homes brandishing a towel or curtain over the door.[104] It was sort of an ancient vacancy sign for feast-time accommodations. Throughout the hilltop streets, visitors encountered the aroma of swirling market spices and the scent of baking matzah. And, unmistakably, they heard the bleating cries of everyone's Passover lambs. While guests and family members shopped for bitter herbs, bread, and wine, the heads of each household led their Passover lambs to the Temple for inspection.[105] In four short days, during the twilight hours leading into the feast, the cries of those lambs and the songs of the people would mingle together in the ancient symphony of sacrifice.

Two thousand years later, with the Temple utterly destroyed and my people globally dispersed, we now observe the Passover differently. Without the Jerusalem altar, the symphony of sacrifice is silent, and our ordered remembrances are scattered far and wide. Instead of feasting on bean stew, fresh olives, and juicy dates, we dine on matzah ball soup, gefilte fish, and coconut macaroons.*

*Lorenzi, *Jesus's Last Supper Menu*. For the uninitiated, gefilte fish are giant meatballs made from chopped up white fish and can be purchased premade in jars of

Yet, for as many differences as there are in the way we celebrate Passover today, there are many similarities to the ancient pilgrim gatherings in Jerusalem.[106] It's shocking, really, how much remains the same. Reclining at our full tables, we still share four cups of wine—two cups before the meal and two afterwards—recalling the same four redemption promises of God. We still break unleavened bread and dip bitter herbs before the dinner break. Children still launch the retelling—to much cheer and adulation—by asking specific questions about what makes Passover "different from all other nights." Even our singing of the Hallel psalms remains split in two by the dinner meal itself. The predinner praises look back toward the exodus redemption, and the postdinner psalms look ahead to God's faithfulness in bringing the Israelites to Jerusalem—and ultimately to messianic redemption.[107] In the words of one modern rabbi, "Messianic hope inspires the singing from [after the dinner break] through the completion of the seder."[108]

Indeed, every time my people have gathered around the Passover table, we have been taught to take in the historical exodus redemption with an eye toward eternal redemption. We are even taught to expect the Messiah's arrival on Passover, because the greater redemption is supposed to take place on the anniversary of the first.[109] And so, with the after-dinner Hallel psalms, we begin shifting our gaze toward the coming Messiah. We beckon Elijah to join us at the table, looking toward God's promise to set eternal redemption in motion with the return of the prophet.[110]

> Behold, I will send you Elijah the prophet before
>   the great
> and awesome day of the Lord comes.
>
> (Mal. 4:5 ESV; 3:23 in Jewish Scriptures)

---

jellied fish broth. With deepest apologies to my Grandpa Jud, I would readily trade that eastern European creation for first-century bean stew any day.

Ever since Malachi, we've been sitting at the Passover table like watchmen on top of Jerusalem's wall, hoping that *this* will finally be the year of eternal redemption. This Passover longing eventually grew into ritual. In Temple times, people began to pour a cup of Passover wine for Elijah, and during the Middle Ages, people started opening the door for him.[111] Both are now fully integrated into the present-day Passover seder.

For as far back as I can remember, inviting Elijah into our midst has been my favorite moment of the evening. It happens near the very end of the seder, when we're all a bit sleepy from rich food and hours of sitting. But in this magical moment, our senses sharpen. Together we rise—not to leave, but to honor Elijah and beckon him back to the earth for his promised mission. Hushed and watching from the table, we keep our eyes glued to the lucky one chosen that night to get up and open wide the front door. I remember holding my breath at this moment growing up, thinking year after year that this might just be the night when the great prophet would come striding through the door. Maybe, after being greeted by the lucky door opener—*Baruch haba! Welcome!*—Elijah would come sit down in our astonished midst and lift high his goblet, filled to the brim with sweet Manischewitz![112] Why *not* that year, after all?

And so, with doors open wide, the Jewish people sing our invitation to Elijah every year, the same melody rippling around the globe. The simple song expresses a collective longing for the restoration of all that is broken, as well as trust in Adonai's promise-keeping. And though we are to trust His timing, our invitation is laced with hope that this time might finally be *the* time.

> *Eliyahu haNavi, Eliyahu HaTishbi, Elyahu Hagiladi,*
> *Bimherah Yavo Elenu Im Mashiach Ben David.*
> Elijah the prophet, Elijah the Tishbite from Gilead;
> he will soon be in our midst, accompanying the
> Messiah, son of David.

Every year of my childhood, I was absolutely certain that Elijah had been there, ever so briefly, among us there in Brooklyn. I was certain because, as the front door stood ajar, the wine in Elijah's cup would begin to slosh. My eyes would grow like saucers. I didn't know why Elijah wouldn't let himself be seen, but I just *knew* he had been with us. Eventually, of course, I realized that it had been my grandpa all along, nudging the table with his knee to stir up our wonder. He loved seeing the delight in our young faces at the prospect of the prophet's arrival. As much as this truth made perfect sense, I was disappointed to realize it. But with each Passover that the door closed, leaving Elijah's chair empty, God's people did not close the door to hope. Our ancient anticipation simply grew, year after year.

All of these remembrances and longings are what Jesus stepped into when He arrived in Jerusalem for His final Passover. He stepped into Israel's remembrance of so much blood dripping from doorposts as death passed us over. He stepped into Israel's remembrance of God's mighty, outstretched arm providing a way when there was no way. And He stepped into Israel's desperate hope, swelling greater with each year, that the promised Messiah would arrive on this anniversary of redemption, rescuing us once and for all. Jesus shouldered the weight of all these remembrances and longings as He entered Jerusalem for the very last time, because they are exactly why He had come. And with God's holy city filled to the brim, millions of pilgrims would watch redemption unfold. Hope was on its way.

I am desperately grateful to now know this hope fulfilled, to know the Messiah and His greater redemption. I am also desperately grateful to know the restoration of some of the dearest, deepest relationships of my life. Sharing that Passover meal together in my grandparents' home was an incredible gift. There we were, reunited around a table for the very first time since we had pilgrimaged together to Jerusalem. And, just like

Jerusalem's ancient pilgrim population grew in number as time passed, so had ours. Four generations now gathered around the table of redemption in my grandparents' sunroom. And it was sweeter than any almond cake my grandma ever served.

Jerusalem calls us to heal.

CHAPTER 8

Redemption's Table

In my distress I called to the LORD, and he answered me.
Psalm 120:1 ESV

Hosanna!

Hosanna?

I sat in the dark on the hotel bathroom floor, surrounded by bathing suits dripping with Dead Sea saltwater. Holding my borrowed travel Bible with one hand, I aimed my flashlight with the other. These were the quaint days before the existence of smartphones loaded with flashlights and Bible apps. I was on that post-Palmyra trip with my family, engrossed in my nighttime pilgrimage routine of reading John's Gospel in the pitch dark after everyone else had fallen asleep.

In those quiet minutes alone each night, I took in Jesus for the very first time. I watched Him rise from each page and walk the very same dusty roads my family was walking. Everything about Him—His words, His touch, His friends—was brand-new to me. I felt like a toddler must feel upon studying a spring leaf for the very first time: pure, newfound wonder. I drank in every drop of this living water, quenching a thirst I never knew I had. Then, each morning, sleepy-eyed from my late-night banned-book reading, I watched each narrative spring to life before my eyes. I explored Jesus's homeland from Bethlehem to Jerusalem and everywhere in between. I've never gotten over God's kindness to give me that time in the Holy Land just seven days after Palmyra.

The night before our Dead Sea swimming, John 11 had wowed me with the apostle's description of Lazarus stepping out of his tomb, four days after his burial, at the mere words of Jesus. I marveled at the thought of Lazarus's death clothes unraveling from his body, which was now very much alive. The wonder of it left me hungry for more. But I wasn't prepared for Jesus's arrival in Jerusalem for my favorite feast: Passover. *Hosanna*? Palm branches? On the *ground*? I knew this. But not *here*. *It's all wrong*, I thought, with an arrogance known to plague baby believers. *These Christians have messed things up. Palm branches and hosannas are not for Passover. They belong at the Feast of Booths.*

I rolled my eyes. Not at Jesus, but at those Christians who seemed to be forever twisting Jewish things around. Soon enough, I would realize that those palm branches on the ground of Jerusalem's hillside weren't a mistake at all. I would comprehend that even palm branches were being made new. At that point in my baby faith, though, I had no idea what was coming during that Passover week. Yes, I believed that Jesus was real and true and had come as the Messiah. But I didn't know the gospel. I knew, in very generic terms, that Jesus had died to pay the price for sin, but I hadn't read what Jesus would actually endure. I didn't know what He had endured for *me*.

Of course, if I had remembered my own Jewish history, I would have known that Hanukkah's victorious Maccabees had waved palm branches in celebration when they reclaimed Jerusalem from Syrian occupation (1 Macc. 13:51). I would have known that, in the two centuries between that day and the hosannas on the hillside, palm branches had become a symbol of Jewish victory. If I had known my Jewish history better, I would have also known that for every Passover while the Temple stood, Jerusalem's residents came out of the city to welcome the weary pilgrims as they approached.[113] I would have recognized the traditional Passover greeting on their lips—the liturgy from Psalm 118, the last of the Hallel psalms. I would have known that the Jerusalemites and the pilgrims were greeting each other in song with the psalmist's exclamation: "Blessed is he who comes in the name of the Lord" (Ps. 118:26 NIV). And that they were echoing the joyous lyrics, beckoning everyone to join the festal procession with boughs in hand. "Save us we pray!" they cried on the way toward celebrating the exodus. "Hosanna!"

If I had known or remembered these things, then Jesus's entry into Jerusalem would have felt beautifully familiar to my Jewish sensibilities. Yet, the whole thing still seemed off. It felt like these people were going totally off script. And I knew I wasn't alone in thinking so, because the Pharisees who had come to welcome the multitudes asked Jesus to rebuke them for saying such things (Luke 19:39).

But Jesus refused to quiet them. He refused because the people weren't going off script at all. They were simply ready to step into the next act, the one everyone had been waiting for. They were embracing the annual hope that the Messiah would come rescue Israel at Passover. Could it be that the people on the hillside had taken to heart their palm-branch memories from the last and greatest day of the Feast of Booths? Were they remembering how they had thrown their fronds to the ground and cried out for salvation around the altar? Surely they had been pondering Jesus's claims to be the Light of the World and the source of living water—that is to say, God Himself. Maybe they now believed that this might finally be the year when God would bring the greater redemption. If it was, they knew exactly what they were supposed to look for.

> Like the initial redeemer, so will be the ultimate redeemer: Just as regarding the initial redeemer, it is stated: "Moses took his wife and his sons, and mounted them on the donkey" (Exod. 4:20), so too, regarding the ultimate redeemer it is stated: "[Your king is coming to you . . .] humble and riding on a donkey."
>
> (Zech. 9:9, *Kohelet Rabbah* 1:9)

At the sight of the Teacher entering Jerusalem on the back of a borrowed donkey, palm branches and hosannas rained down. For so long, Israel had been watching for the ultimate Redeemer to arrive, humble and riding on a donkey. They had been waiting for this exact sign for five hundred years. Now here it was, happening at Passover just like they had always been taught by the priests, scribes, and Pharisees. The people on the pilgrim road understood exactly what this moment would mean. Their cries of "Save us, son of David!" were filled with the fervor of people seeking the promise and of recognizing the Promised One—even if they didn't fully understand it, or Him, yet.

Oh, how wrong I had been about all those passion-week hosannas! This wasn't a confusion of Jewish customs at all. The hilltop hosannas and palm fronds were a public response to the whispers and wonderings about Jesus's deity. People were connecting their Feast of Booths cries of salvation—those palm-branch hosannas around the altar—to the humble arrival of the One who had offered them all living water. This was the beginning of faith, blooming on that springtime hill of Mount Zion.

The liturgical greetings of God's love and salvation filled the air until the road reached its turn at the Mount of Olives. There, the splendor of Jerusalem came into full view. And with the hosannas still ringing in His ears, Jesus wept. Not with a simple shedding of tears like the ones He had cried at Lazarus's temporary tomb.* No, as Jesus looked out over the City of Peace,

**Dakryō* means to shed tears (Blue Letter Bible Lexicon).

He lamented with deep grief (Luke 19:41).** He mourned under the weight of His burden, looking out over the city He loved, filled with the people He loved, with the foreboding plateau of Golgotha jutting out from the hillside. Jesus knew that in a matter of days, Jerusalem would break His body and His heart on that very stretch of barren rock. Jesus knew that *all* of us would break His body and His heart in that place. And He wept bitterly. The sight of the City of Peace brought anything but peace in those moments. The hopes and fears of all the years accelerated toward fulfillment.

Pushing past the tears and the hosannas, Jesus entered the city, where worshipers busied themselves with the day's task. The feast may have been four days away, but there was a very specific job to be done on this particular day, the tenth of Nisan. It was the day that each household of Israel was to identify their lamb for the Passover sacrifice (Exod. 12:3). Rabbis explained that God assigned this date because four days were needed to observe the lambs and confirm that they were, indeed, perfect and fit for sacrifice.[114] Even this seemingly insignificant detail brimmed with prophetic significance: The day that everyone was selecting their Passover lambs was the very same day the pilgrims on the hillside hailed Jesus as the One who saves. I remember when this connection first registered in my mind. I looked up from my Bible and exclaimed wildly, to no one but myself: *Are you kidding me?* Palm Sunday is *literally* lamb selection day.

Just like all the sacrificial lambs in Jerusalem, Jesus was being examined every minute of these four days, too. Each morning, He left His festal home base in Bethany to teach at the Temple Mount (Matt. 21:17). Without anything official to do until the day of sacrifice, crowds would gather there every

***Klaiō* means to mourn, weep, or lament outwardly as one who grieves for the dead (Blue Letter Bible Lexicon).

day. Now, those crowds gathered and considered Jesus's words. Of course, the pilgrims weren't the only ones watching Jesus during those four days. The chief priests, too, watched Him preach, prophesy, and purify. Scribes took notes as He foretold destruction and resurrection. Leaders witnessed Him flipping tables and dispensing woes. The joint conclusion of Jesus's opposition was that He was worthy of sacrifice. They were right, of course, but for all the wrong reasons. They agreed, though, that Passover was not the right time to act—not with Jerusalem teeming with two to three million pilgrims who were amazed and hanging on Jesus's every word.[115] It seemed to the priests and Pharisees that the entire world had gone after him (John 12:19).

As much as the religious leadership were worried about Jesus's threat to their power structures, though, they were more worried about upsetting Rome. The whole city was under a Roman microscope that week. The Passover crowds had grown so large over the years that the empire had started beefing up its military presence at the Jerusalem garrison just for this feast.[116] Because of this, Jesus's adversaries thought it best to deal with Him once Passover had ended and His adoring fans left town (Matt. 26:3–5).

By the eve of the feast, though, all of Jerusalem had turned to busying themselves with preparations for their seders. Jesus and the Twelve were no exception. Jesus shifted His attention from teaching the crowds in the courts to sharing with His friends around the Passover table. It seems that a follower in the city had offered a furnished room, so Jesus sent John and Peter into Jerusalem to make preparations (Matt. 26:17–19; Mark 14:12–16; Luke 22:7–13). Off they scurried into the smells of baking bread, simmering stew, and dying lambs. The sights, sounds, and smells of the twilight Passover slaughter were like nothing we can comprehend. There on the Temple Mount, hundreds of thousands of perfect lambs played their part in the retelling of that terrifying night in Egypt—that night when the cries of lambs gave way to the wails of mourning.

It's difficult for my modern brain to fathom that scene of sacrifice. Row after row of people stepped forward in unison, each with a lamb in tow, until their line met the row of waiting priests. There, each worshiper cut the throat of his household's lamb as the priest caught the blood in a basin. Basin after basin of lambs' blood passed backward toward the altar, from the hands of one priest to another, until the last one poured it out at the base of the massive bronze structure. Emptied, the basins were passed back up to the front line of priests, ready for the next row of offerors.[117] It was a bloody assembly line, staining hands and feet and altar to a soundtrack of bleating lambs and chanted praises. Levites and worshipers sang and proclaimed the Hallel psalms on a loop—with all their hosannas and hallelujahs—until the very last lamb gave up its very last breath.[118] For all its spiritual beauty, Passover was a horribly messy business.

Most of those lambs had drawn their very *first* breath in Bethlehem, just like King David had almost a millennia earlier. Now, the Son of David—the Lamb of God also born in Bethlehem—made His way through Jerusalem to the upper room as the sun sank lower. How Jesus's chest must have tightened with every refrain of "Hosanna!" that drifted above the cries of dying lambs. Come tomorrow, that would be Him: broken and emptied, answering all the people's hosannas—their repeated pleas of "Save, we pray."[119] Did His heart tremble, His mind race, His stomach churn? Or did Jesus push it all aside to focus on this last night of fellowship with His friends?

By now, they were all on their way to the upper room, too. John and Peter were probably roasting the lamb, their feet crusted with the blood and dust of Passover. Each and every moment in that upper room is a gift to unwrap. At that table of abundance, Jesus spoke the old Passover remembrances and made them new. With every whisper of redemption and grace, He gathered the ancient threads of Passover liturgy and stitched us all together into one redeemed people. With words we still recount in churches today, Jesus launched the greater, forever exodus.

That evening, instead of the ceremonial hand washing at the Passover table, Jesus got up and washed everyone's feet. He showed these dear friends how to serve and to love. Jesus demonstrated how deeply and tenderly He cared for each of them—even the one He knew would betray Him (Matt. 26:14–15, 25; John 13:2, 26).

When Jesus called His friends to order—that is, to *seder*—they all reclined at the table filled with bounty by Peter and John. The unleavened bread and bitter herbs and roasted lamb filled the candlelit room with the rich aroma of Passover. The Teacher raised the first cup in unison with every single host throughout all Jerusalem. Parents, children, and friends old and new reclined on cushions around their low tables, propping themselves up on their left side.[120] I imagine they looked up expectantly at their host in the same way I always looked up at my own grandpas: with bright eyes and a wide smile. The whole hillside blessed that first Passover cup in a concert of blessing, chanting the same words in their separate spaces, united in the shadow of God's earthly dwelling.

As always, the nation set apart and elevated their Passover worship with the blessing of that first cup, *Kadesh*—the cup of sanctification. But Jesus began that unforgettable evening by pouring the first cup of Passover for the very last time. Jesus's companions would eventually understand that He was not just elevating the annual Passover table above all other tables of the year. Jesus was elevating this *specific* Passover table above all other Passover tables ever—even the celebrated ones of the Egypt escape.

Pouring the second cup, the cup of retelling, Jesus began leading the disciples toward a new retelling. But first, like all of Jerusalem around them, the thirteen embarked on the familiar narrative, recounting everything that had transpired to bring God's people out from the oppression of Egypt. Leading their remembrance, Jesus recalled the bitter bondage and the burning bush, the hardened Pharaoh and the mounting plagues, the bloodied doorposts and the midnight wailing, the hasty departure and the splitting sea. Around the table, His companions remembered together as they always did, and as we Jews still do—as people who had been there. By God's command, they saw, heard, and tasted every harrowing moment of suffering and liberation as if it had happened to each of them (Exod. 13:8).[121]

As they recounted the hurried, late-night flight from Egypt, Jesus raised the unleavened bread for them all to see. He held up that bread of affliction, as God had named it, just like my grandpas always did and just like grandpas were doing all across Jerusalem that night. With the matzah lifted high, they recounted together the distress of Egypt and the rushed escape to which that bread was meant to bear witness (Deut. 16:3). Then, in the warmth of the upper room, Jesus told the disciples that from that day forward, whenever they held this bread of affliction in their hands, they must also remember something new. He told his friends to see the Passover table in ways they had never imagined: to remember not only the bread of the ancient exodus but the broken bread of His own body (Matt. 26:26; Mark 14:22).

Confusion surely rushed in. It had made perfect sense to them that, the day after feeding the five thousand, Jesus had declared Himself to be the Bread of Life (John 6). On that mountaintop in Galilee, people began to recognize Him as the promised prophet, the messianic manna foretold by the rabbis (John 6:14).[122] But here at their Passover table, Jesus wasn't talking about multiplied loaves or wafers sweet as honey. No, the bread breaking in Jesus's hands was the bread of affliction.

This—the bread of suffering, poverty, and refugees—*is my body*. Could this be just another parable? A hard saying? They were too afraid or too embarrassed to ask Him to explain. Whatever the nature of the disciples' confusion in that moment, it would only increase as the evening continued.

In the middle of the seder—that hinge of symmetry in the Passover worship—Jesus and the disciples paused to eat the meal that John and Peter had set before them. They ate their fill, feasting together on Jerusalem's bounty and on the Passover lamb, sacrificed just hours earlier. And then, turning back to their worship, Jesus raised the after-dinner cup in concert with every other host in the city. He offered thanksgiving for the meal they had just eaten and poured the blood of grapes into their cups for the third time (Mark 14:23; Luke 22:20).[123] They remembered together the blood of the first Passover. They recalled the blood of the Nile, the blood of the lambs, and the blood of our brethren spilled in slavery. And just as He had done with the unleavened bread before dinner, Jesus went deeper.

The Messiah raised the third cup with His steady right hand and recalled God's third promise in Exodus 6, like they had always done—like we still do: "I will redeem you with an outstretched arm." Jesus told the disciples to remember something new about this third cup, something new about God's redemption. And while some traditions call it the "cup of grace" and others the "cup of redemption," this after-dinner cup is filled with the reality of both. In the hands of Jesus that night, it began to overflow: "This cup is the new covenant in My blood, which is shed for you" (Luke 22:20 NKJV). The new covenant would be sealed with blood, just like the first covenant had been sealed with blood on Sinai's altar (Exod. 24:1–8). Only, not like it at all. This new covenant would be sealed not with the blood of bulls but with the holy blood of heaven. From that day forward, the third cup would be taken not only in remembrance of countless lambs and dripping doorframes but of the one Lamb and a dripping crossbeam. No longer would the blood of the Passover cover Israel alone, but it would be poured out for the salvation of all humanity (Matt. 26:28; Mark 14:24).[124]

The *new covenant*. Jesus had finally said it out loud, as clear as day. Here at the Passover table, that ancient feast of redemption, Jesus was ushering in the greater redemption, the greater exodus, and the greater freedom. In a matter of hours, He would seal it with His own body and blood. And on the other side of it all, the disciples would look back and remember, just as Jesus had told them to do. His mysterious words would eventually make perfect, painful sense. The disciples would finally fathom that, in that upper room, Jesus had changed everything about the Passover remembrance. Indeed, He was making all things new: new bread, new wine, and a new covenant. But on that blissfully ignorant Thursday evening, the disciples got up from that meal feeling confident and loved. And, pledging allegiance to their leader, they walked out into the night.

The whole city, in fact, was spilling outside as it neared midnight, merging back together into a sea of humanity cascading over the mountaintop.* Most people climbed up onto rooftops, where they turned toward the Temple and sang the Hallels one last time, this time under the light of the full silvery moon.[125] Millions of redeemed voices, young and old, sang so many hallelujahs. They simply had no idea, in the middle of such mirth and worship, just how redeemed they were about to become.

Singing those same verses and hallelujahs, Jesus led His friends outside, too. But instead of scrambling up to the rooftops, they climbed the Mount of Olives, following Jesus to the garden of Gethsemane (Matt. 26:30, 36; Mark 14:26, 32). He knew exactly what awaited them there. In a matter of minutes, the leisurely reclining and earnest fellowship of the upper

*The Passover worship meal is to be completed before midnight, because it was at midnight that the final plague—death of the firstborn—made its way through Egypt (see Exodus 12:29; B. Pesachim 120b).

room would give way to dizzying chaos and crippling fear. The disciples would seem to be caught in a slow-motion nightmare. Drops of sweat and blood. The betrayer's kiss. A severed ear. Arrest. Desertion. Kangaroo court. Denial, denial, denial. Torture. Death. Jesus could see it all coming as they made their way up the Mount of Olives. Even if He had tried to block it out, the Hallels they all sang under the stars proclaimed what lay before Him—especially Psalm 116. The psalmist's words formed a highlight reel of flashbacks and flash-forwards, as Jesus and the disciples made their way up to Gethsemane, the "olive press."

The psalm rose from Jesus's lips and the lips of all Jerusalem, filling the night:

> I love the Lord, for He has heard my voice—my appeal for mercy.
> Because He has inclined His ear to me, I will call on Him as long as I live.
> The ropes of death entangled me; the anguish of Sheol overcame me;
> I was confronted by trouble and sorrow.
> Then I called on the name of the Lord: "O Lord, deliver my soul!"
> The Lord is gracious and righteous; our God is full of compassion.
> The Lord preserves the simplehearted; I was helpless, and He saved me.
> Return to your rest, O my soul, for the Lord has been good to you.
> For You have delivered my soul from death, my eyes from tears, my feet from stumbling.
> I will walk before the Lord in the land of the living.
> I believed, therefore I said, "I am greatly afflicted."
> In my alarm I said, "All men are liars!"
> How can I repay the Lord for all His goodness to me?

I will lift the cup of salvation and call on the name of
the Lord.
I will fulfill my vows to the Lord in the presence of all
His people.
Precious in the sight of the Lord is the death of
His saints.
Truly, O Lord, I am Your servant; I am Your servant,
the son of Your maidservant;
You have broken my bonds.
I will offer to You a sacrifice of thanksgiving and call on
the name of the Lord.
I will fulfill my vows to the Lord in the presence of all
His people,
in the courts of the Lord's house, in your midst, O
Jerusalem.
Hallelujah!

(Ps. 116 BSB)

In just a matter of hours, Jesus would fulfill His vows in the presence of all God's people. There, in the midst of Jerusalem, the Messiah drank the cup of salvation. As the ropes of death tightened around the Son of God, they must have entangled God's maidservant, too. *Oh, Mary, mother of God.* Did her wailing fill the air, there at the splintering cross? The sword was piercing Mary's very soul, just as Simeon had said it would, back on that beautiful day in the shadow of the Temple, when her baby was just one month old (Luke 2:34–35).

Just the day before, those throngs of people had been pressed together in the Temple courts, sacrificing Passover lambs in wave after wave, blood pouring out in steady streams of remembrance. Now, the One whom so many had hailed with victory palms and hosannas was bleeding before their eyes. Bleeding from His head, His hands, His feet. Everything foretold in the private upper room was now playing out in the public square. The One called the Lamb of God was being broken and emptied for all the world to see (John 1:29). But this was why Jesus had come, after all. And God had beckoned the whole nation to pilgrimage and bear witness to His sacrifice. It may have been the intention of Jesus's enemies to hide the crucifixion, but it was God's intention to magnify it (Matt. 26:2–5).

Gentiles from Rome, Jews from Babylon, and everyone in between watched the Lamb of God offered up that day. They watched with their own eyes as He took on the full weight of the world, gasping for air and gulping down the cup of our redemption to the very last drop. The pilgrims would remember it all with scarred eyes and troubled minds. Of course, they would later learn about the bread and wine in the upper room and about the covenant made new. But they would also never forget the sight of the Teacher dying in the middle of the pressing crowd. They would remember familiar voices, even their own, swept up in the horrible fervor. They would remember the taunts and sobs and stunned faces. And they would describe it all to friends and acquaintances when they traveled back home. They would always remember what redemption had cost.

I remember, too—in that ancient Passover way. Just as I grew up remembering the exodus as though I had labored under the Pharaoh, sheltered under the blood, and scrambled through the waters, I now also remember as a friend at Jesus's table and a woman witnessing the cross. I know that I, too, am crusted with the blood and dust of Passover, in desperate need of cleansing. I hear myself, too, betraying, abandoning, and denying. When I close my eyes, I see the Lamb bleeding under the weight of my sin, suffocating under the gravity of things I've done and of things done to me. And, becoming a witness to my redemption through my remembering, I am spellbound by His mighty outstretched arms, parting the deep to gather me up—to gather *all* of us up.

Even now, when I take the bread and the wine, my breath sometimes catches and my eyes brim. Because when we are called to remember the Redeemer's words at the Last Supper, I find myself transported to the upper room and to Golgotha's rock. I can't help but picture Jesus's perfect human hands breaking fresh-baked matzah just hours before they were pierced. I can't help but picture Him lifting high the cup of redemption and giving thanks just hours before being lifted up in sacrifice. No matter how many times I ponder it, the thought of my Messiah, broken, bloodied, poured out, and all alone is so desperately heavy; it's too much to bear sometimes.

But that is when I choose to also remember the hosanna palm branches—the ones I used to think were all wrong. I picture those vibrant green fronds that are literally the Hebrew root of my very own name: *Tamar*, palm branch. I visualize myself as one of those branches, not only falling at Jesus's feet on the springtime hillside but also now waving in His victory. I remember that I have chosen my Lamb and that He has chosen me. *Hosanna!*

Jerusalem calls us to remember.

CHAPTER 9

Risen Bread

They who sow in tears shall reap with songs of joy.
Psalm 126:5 JPS85

Graveyards don't usually conjure up feelings of wonder in young adolescents. At least they didn't in thirteen-year-old me. But this particular cemetery was like nothing I had ever seen. Endless rows of sun-bleached markers scaled the sprawling hillside. A mix of polished and crumbling slabs fanned out in sections from the bottom of the Mount of Olives all the way up to its summit, interrupted here and there by a stone mausoleum or a soaring cypress. To my eyes, the gravestones—stacked and overlapped in tier after tier—looked like an ancient, macabre stadium.

My grandparents and I stood there with the rest of our group and listened to the Middle Eastern lilt of our young guide's perfect English. Amatziah—his name meaning "God is strong"—told us that upwards of 150,000 people are buried on that rocky slope. But it wasn't the size or the structure of the cemetery that boggled my brain. Amatziah swept his arm across our view of the vista, excitedly explaining that the very first people buried there were from the early years of David's reign, back when Israel's second king established Jerusalem as the capital three thousand years ago. The oldest markers identify the resting places of King David's son Absolom as well as the great prophets Haggai, Zachariah, and Malachi.[126] It was one thing to see ancient buildings and artifacts, but beholding the graves of ancient people whose words fill the Scriptures left me awestruck.

Just as intriguing to me was the sight of modern graves dotting the hillside. People are still being buried on the Mount of Olives, sharing the same resting place as famed prophets and sons of kings. Of course, not just anybody can be buried there now. There isn't room for ordinary folk. (If there were, my loved ones might have to come to Jerusalem to visit my bones one day.) But significant Jewish leaders, authors, and rabbis from modern days are laid to rest there, as are a British and a Danish monarch and a victim of 9/11.[127]

The ancient cemetery offers a beautiful view of the Kidron Valley below. But that isn't why the Mount of Olives is a prized burial site. I learned from Amatziah that the people laid to rest on the Mount of Olives hillside are said to be the very first to rise when the Messiah arrives. This does make sense, since it faces the Temple Mount. The dead are even buried there with their feet toward the Temple, making their resurrected walk toward the Holy Place all the more swift.[128]

To be perfectly honest, Amatziah's talk of resurrection was pretty foreign to me. None of the Jews I had known talked about the resurrection of the dead—not even my Messiah-anticipating grandparents. I'm not sure why. Some rabbis say it's because there is nothing to do about it while we're still living on this side of death. But, lest someone try to convince you that Judaism isn't anchored in the resurrection of the dead, know that the Mishnah declares that to deny it is to commit heresy.[129] What makes it heretical is that it denies the fundamental nature of

God: He is absolutely good and just. Without resurrection, the triumphs of evil on the earth would have the last word, making God unjust and lacking in power.[130] Instead, the reality of resurrection means that death is not the end of our story. It means that our lives continue beyond death simply as the next stage of our life. There is technically no afterlife in Judaism, only the *continuation* of life—the same life lived in the higher realms, in incorruptible bodies, amid incorruptible love, and with the incorruptible God. The people buried on the Mount of Olives, many of whom died at the hands of tragedy and evil, anchored their trust in the inevitability of God's justice and in His eternal goodness.

Of course, I didn't grasp most of that as a thirteen-year-old standing in the middle of Mount Zion's ancient graveyard. Instead, my mind flooded with images of what the mountain might look like on the day of Messiah's arrival. Honestly, it both fascinated and spooked me. For the rest of our trip, every time our adventures took us within eyeshot of that tiered hillside, I imagined what it would look like one day, overflowing with the resurrected bodies of the ancients. Once I left the Holy Land, though, my imaginings of the mass reawakening dissipated. Those resurrection visions seemed to belong to a different time and place once I reentered the modern sights and sensibilities of the United States. There was nothing I could do to hasten the day of that mass resurrection, anyway.

Back home, whenever that limestone-layered hillside came to mind, I thought about the more graspable things I had learned about the Kidron Valley. So much used to happen in that lush expanse between the Mount of Olives and Jerusalem—including a harvest ritual during the Passover feast. That ritual was something that a teenager growing up in the cornbread basket of the nation could relate to. Little did I know back then that Jerusalem's quiet grain ceremony, originally prescribed by God in the dust of the wilderness, would become inextricably linked to the resurrection of Jesus, and that I would come to believe it.

In the days of the Temple, this harvest ritual began on the very same day that all of Jerusalem was scurrying to and fro, gathering, baking, slaughtering, and roasting. Leaving the hustle and bustle of the city's seder preparations, three delegates from the Sanhedrin walked across the Kidron Valley to the edge of a golden barley field, ripe for the harvest.

> Tell the Israelites: When you come to the land I am going to give you and you harvest grain, bring the priest a bundle of the first grain you harvest. He will present it to the LORD so that you will be accepted. He will present it on the day after Passover. *
>
> (Lev. 23:10–11 GW)

Barley was the first crop to ripen in Israel. And the barley fields in the fertile valley of the Kidron Brook were perfect for this special offering. Crops there required no irrigation or fertilization, which was significant because those farming practices were specifically forbidden for the firstfruits offering.[131] The firstfruits waved before the Eternal were to be untouched by human ingenuity, allowed to flourish by God's provision alone. Another requirement was that the stalks were to remain firmly rooted in the ground until the sickle sliced through them on the afternoon before the offering. The barley would be farm fresh, straight from the ripened field to the Temple table. So,

*Most translations render this phrase as "the sabbath," rather than "the day after Passover." That is technically correct. However, in the context of this section of Leviticus, God is referring to Nisan 15, the first night of the Passover. Feast days that call for a cessation of all other activities are referred to as a sabbath. These verses are preceded by God's commands for Passover, which refers to the feast itself as "a sabbath." Sabbath literally means an "intermission," which I think is a beautiful way to think about our weekly day of rest, as well as the feast days on which we are meant to pause everything to worship and meditate on God.

while the elders didn't harvest the barley that day, they did go ahead and mark the stalks necessary to yield the prescribed amount of grain. Loosely tied in manageable sections, the barley stalks stood waving in the valley breeze, organized and ready for reaping.

The three elders would return to the field the next afternoon at twilight, each one armed with a sickle and basket.[132] It would now be twenty-four hours since the twilight sacrifice of the nation's Passover lambs. Setting out on their mission through the valley, the three always attracted an audience of locals, who received them with great fanfare on their way to the stalks.[133] Upon reaching the edge of the field, the elders would ask a series of questions to the crowd, repeating each query twice, to which the assembly would cry out in the affirmative.[134]

> Did the sun set? Yes! Did the sun set? Yes!
> Shall I reap the sheaves with this sickle? Yes! With this sickle? Yes!
> Shall I place the gathered sheaves in this basket? Yes! In this basket? Yes!
> Shall I cut the sheaves? Cut! Shall I cut the sheaves? Cut!

And with that, the three blades sliced through the ripened stalks, felling them in their perfect bundles. The elders placed the bales in their baskets and carried the barley back up the hill, to the eastern side of the Temple courtyard.[135] There, priests received the harvested barley and began the long process of preparing the flour for the morning offering. They beat the stalks with soft reeds and cabbage stalks instead of the usual sticks, gently separating the kernels so they wouldn't be crushed through the process.[136] After roasting the separated grain, the priests spread it out to cool and dry in the courtyard wind.[137]

The barley was finally ready to be ground into flour. The priests first ground the kernels in a gristmill. Then, measuring out a half pound of the coarse flour (one tenth of an ephah), they passed it through a series of thirteen sieves, the holes of each successive screen growing smaller and smaller. Verifying that the barley flour was fine enough for this special wave offering, one of the priests would plunge his hand in and out of the bowl, making sure that not a bit of it clung to him.[138] Once approved, the superfine flour rested in safekeeping until morning. All throughout this sacred milling process, the rest of Jerusalem worshiped at their seder tables and sang psalms on the rooftops.

At daybreak, while the city slowly began to wake from its post-seder slumber, a designated priest made his way into the courtyard. Chosen to offer up the barley firstfruits on behalf of the gathered nation, he took the vessel of flour, added a measure of olive oil and frankincense, and kneaded the mixture to create a fragrant dough. Reminiscent of the bundled branches that the pilgrims waved during the Feast of Booths a few months earlier, the priest now lifted the vessel toward the corner of the altar and waved the dough in all four directions: north, south, east, and west. Once again, Israel collectively confessed their complete dependence on the God of all creation, this time through the priest's waving on their behalf. He waved horizontally, praying for protection over their crops from "destructive winds," and then waved vertically, praying against damage from "injurious dews."[139] Now having waved the barley, or "omer," in all directions before the altar, the priest withdrew a handful of the dough and threw it onto the fire.[140] And with that offering of the grain firstfruits, all the nation's barley crops were released for harvest and consumption.[141]

That ancient offering of the barley firstfruits is a meaningful ritual authored by God. Yet it so often gets lost in the celebration of Passover, at least in modern minds. The meticulous preparation of stalks, grain, and dough becomes overshadowed by the large-scale preparation of lambs, bread, and wine—especially because our Passover celebrations continue today, while the omer offering does not. But they were equally commanded, and I find a beauty in God's call to couple them together.

That beauty was marred, however, during one particular omer offering: the morning after Jesus died. While the priest was waving the fragrant dough through the air, watched by worshipers in the Temple court, Jesus's body lay cold in the dark silence of a rock-cut tomb. And the way His body arrived inside that carved-out limestone paints a contrast just as jarring. It may have felt like ages ago, but it had been less than a day since Jesus had uttered the words, "It is finished" (John 19:30 NIV).

The things that took place after Jesus's last breath often play in my mind like a split-screen movie. Because, as the sun slid toward the horizon that afternoon, two very different groups embarked on two very different missions at the very same time. While the shadows grew longer and the crowds dispersed from Golgotha's spectacle, these two particular groups of people did not head back to their families. They had jobs to do, and they needed to move efficiently in order to complete them before the first three stars appeared in the sky, heralding the official start of the Sabbath.[142]

One of these groups was the delegation of barley reapers. It was time for them to collect their sickles and baskets and to head down into the valley. Making their way across the Kidron Brook, the elders were likely joined by a few teachers and scribes as they walked to the sheaves that stood marked and ready. The meaning of Kidron—"murky" and "dark"—seems most appropriate on that afternoon.

Meanwhile, two other Sanhedrin members walked in the opposite direction of the barley fields. Stepping out from the shadows of their secret faith in Jesus, these two men chose instead to approach the trauma of the cross. One of them boldly asked the Roman governor for permission to bury the crucified body of his rabbi (Mark 15:43).

Down in the valley, at the edge of the barley field, the three elders asked their series of ritual questions, finally ending with, "Shall I cut?" The assembly of bystanders cried out with their ritual refrain: "Cut! Cut!" The three sickles swung through the air in unison, slicing the sheaves to the ground.

Upon Golgotha's rocky plateau, Joseph and Nicodemus slowly lowered the bloodied crossbeam to the ground. Together, they gently unbound their Teacher and removed the iron nails.[143]

The three elders in the barley field shouldered their sickles and lifted their brimming baskets, ready to bear the stalks of grain back across the valley. The ones who had accompanied the elders fell in line behind them.

On the other side of Jerusalem's hill, a few yards from where they had lowered the cross to the ground, the other two elders bore the broken body of Jesus to a garden tomb (John 19:41). Following at a distance as was the custom, a group of grieving women looked on (Luke 23:55; Mark 15:47).[144]

The sheaf bearers finally ascended the holy hill, delivering the fresh bundles of barley to the Temple courtyard into the waiting arms of priests.

Meanwhile, Joseph and Nicodemus carried Jesus's body through the small opening of the rock-hewn tomb, gently laying Him in the carved niche. Stepping back into the waning sunlight, together they pushed the round boulder down its curved channel, closing the resting place of Jesus of Nazareth.[145]

And then it was night. The time for holy yet fitful rest had begun.

The new morning probably did not feel like it brought new mercies for the people who loved Jesus. And since public displays of grief were forbidden on the Sabbath, they grieved behind closed doors.[146] Perhaps Joseph and Nicodemus huddled together in their sadness, relieved to be barred from public interaction after handling Jesus's body (Num. 19:11). Maybe within the privacy of John's family home, Mary wept (John 19:26–27). It does seem like a mercy that everything came to a standstill that day, with no work or travel allowed. Nothing was expected of them that day, and so they rested in their grief.

Eventually the sun set again, bringing the Sabbath to a close. With the dawn of the next day, many of the pilgrims would begin to pack up and say their goodbyes, continuing to observe the Feast of Unleavened Bread along their journey and back in their homes. We know of two people in particular who set off among this first wave of returnees. They embarked on a relatively short journey, just seven miles, to the village of Emmaus. Cleopas and his companion—many scholars believe it was his wife, Mary—made their way down the mountain amid the steady stream of pilgrims.[147] As they talked through the events of the last three days, a stranger startled them, coming alongside the two on the road. This pilgrim shocked them not by his presence but by his apparent oblivion to the dramatic happenings in Jerusalem. "Are you the only visitor to Jerusalem who does not know the things that have happened?" they asked. "What things?" the stranger asked in return (Luke 24:18–19).

What things? How in the world could this man have been in Jerusalem for Passover and not know about the hosannas on the hillside or the crucifixion on Golgotha? So there along the road, the pair of pilgrims told the stranger everything they knew, their words tangled with sadness, confusion, and perhaps glimmers of hope. The two shared about Jesus the Nazarene, recounting His mighty deeds and words over the past three years (Luke 24:19–21). They described how their religious leaders had handed Him over to be crucified by Rome while the whole nation was in Jerusalem for the feast (Luke 24:20). The pilgrims' distress at recounting that day must have darkened their faces. They bemoaned the fact that it was now the third day: that day when the soul leaves the body and a person is, without a single shred of doubt, dead (Luke 24:21).[148] Their hopes for Jesus's redemption of Israel were dashed.

Yet their grief shifted to bewilderment. The two confided in the stranger, telling him about the puzzling happenings of that very morning. Resurrected people had been seen coming out of their tombs and walking into Jerusalem (Matt. 27:52–53). That's something that was only supposed to happen when the Messiah brought redemption.[149] Just as mysterious, some of the women in their fellowship had gone to visit Jesus's tomb that morning, only to find it empty (Luke 24:22–23; Mark 16:3–6).* They had been greeted by an actual angel, waiting for them with incredible news: Jesus had risen, just as He had said. Except none of them had really understood what Jesus meant when He said those words. Two more friends had found the tomb empty, too—except for neatly folded grave clothes (Luke 24:24; John 20:3–8).

Everything seemed so impossible to comprehend that Cleopas and his companion didn't take offense when the stranger called them foolish (Luke 24:25). Maybe they *were* foolish. So they stopped talking and listened. Mile after mile, beginning with Moses and the Prophets, their traveling companion taught them everything they had missed and misunderstood about the suffering and rising Messiah (Luke 24:27). Upon reaching Emmaus, they insisted that their new friend stop and stay with them rather than continuing on his way. It was almost dark, after all, and Jesus had taught them to nourish and shelter strangers (Matt. 25:35). They could honor Him in that way, even now. The stranger accepted their kind invitation.

During their entire journey along the road that day, the eyes of Cleopas and his companion were somehow kept from

*If Cleopas's companion was, indeed, his wife Mary, she would have been one of the women at the tomb that morning, as well as at the cross with the other two Marys (see John 19:25; Boice, "Who Were the Disciples on the Road to Emmaus?," 2019).

recognizing that their new teacher was, in fact, their old teacher—*the* Teacher (Luke 24:16). In the end, it wasn't His words that opened their eyes but His hands. As a guest in their Emmaus home, the learned stranger was invited to bless and break the bread:

> *Baruch atah Adonai, Elohenu Melech Ha'Olam, ha'motzi lechem min ha'aretz.*
> *Blessed are you, Lord our God, King of the Universe, who brings forth bread from the earth.*

Blessed are you, Lord our God, King of the universe, who brought forth Jesus, the Bread of Life, from the earth—quite literally, that very morning. Now, gathered around Cleopas's humble table, Jesus broke unleavened bread with His resurrected hands for the first time. He handed the broken bread of the Passover to His dinner companions in Emmaus, just as He had done with His disciples in the upper room. And it was in that instant—in that moment of breaking and passing the bread of the exodus—that the eyes of Jesus's traveling companions flew open with perfect, staggering clarity. But before they could manage a single, astonished word, the Messiah—now in his glorified body—vanished.

Shock, wonder, and joy propelled the two back to Jerusalem as night began to fall. No longer trudging in heartache but hastening in exhilaration, they pressed their way upstream against the flow of pilgrims leaving the city. Reaching Jerusalem well into the night, the friends burst into the gathering of confused disciples and told them everything: "Were not our hearts burning within us while he talked to us on the road, while he opened to us the Scriptures?" (Luke 24:32 NIV).

Any doubt in the minds of the disciples fell away when Jesus appeared, seemingly out of thin air. The risen Messiah corroborated every claim of the Emmaus pair, every insistence of Peter and John, and every profession of the women simply by His presence among them. He showed them all His hands and His feet, asked for a bite to eat, and opened their minds to understand all they hadn't before (Luke 24:39–48). They stood in amazement and joy. "*Shalom aleichem*," He said to them that night: "Peace be with you" (Luke 24:36 NIV). Peace indeed. Jesus had destroyed the bonds of death, just as God had promised, and now they all saw and understood with unveiled eyes (Isa. 25:8).

Yet even while the eyes and ears of the two from Emmaus were still veiled, they were living out what I believe is the ultimate purpose of the pilgrimage: They were carrying their eyewitness accounts of Jesus—their own faith, hope, and experience—back down the highways and byways. I love the way that the two shared what they knew of Him, incomplete as it was, because it was personal and vulnerable, which is how we're all called to share what we know. In the days to follow, millions of pilgrims would carry their own eyewitness accounts of the Messiah's death and resurrection. Their beautiful feet would carry the good news from the smallest of villages to the most crowded of cities. It would be impossible for anyone to keep the events of this Passover week to themselves. Surely their testimony would spark even more pilgrims to travel back with them to Jerusalem in a couple of months for the next pilgrimage feast. There would be so much more to hear and, hopefully, to see.

I remember reading about the resurrection for the very first time. It was after I returned from my post-Palmyra pilgrimage to the Holy Land. I hadn't made it that far in the Gospel of John during my secret, late-night readings. I hadn't even quite made it to the cross. I was still reading about the hilltop hosannas. But when I finally read the resurrection narratives in the days after my return, I found myself instantly transported to my thirteenth summer, when I had stood in the sprawling Jerusalem cemetery. I remembered my visions of the city swarming with resurrected saints. It had actually *happened*, I just hadn't known it until now. I had now discovered, in the words of Alfred Edersheim, "the innermost shrine in the Sanctuary of [Jesus's] mission."[150] And it is a sanctuary I never, ever want to leave.

I plan to worship in that sanctuary of Jesus's resurrection forever, and to worship in faith until I see Him with my own resurrected eyes. In that moment—the one that Judaism teaches isn't an afterlife at all but the continuation of our current life into eternity—it's said that heaven and earth meet each other in a divine kiss.[151] It's an intoxicating image. And yet, in the most mystifying and breathtaking ways, heaven and earth have already come together. First in the incarnation, as the Shekinah brought the Messiah into our world, and then when the Shekinah drew Him back out of death (Luke 1:35; Rom. 8:11). My heart quickens just thinking about it.

My heart quickens when I ponder the unveiling of the pilgrims' eyes in Emmaus, too. And when I envision their eyes flying open in sudden recognition of Jesus, I can't help but imagine the moment when my own eyes will flicker open to see my Messiah clearly, face-to-face. One day, the dimness of this world will give way in a flash to the brilliance of glory, and my adolescent visions of the Mount of Olives, teeming with resurrected saints and ancestors, will be nothing compared to the magnificent sight of eternity. There, I will become part of an immeasurable multitude of nations and generations, together singing hallelujahs around the very real and risen Lamb, seated on the throne of heaven.

Jerusalem calls us to rise.

CHAPTER 10

Firstfruits Offering

> May the Lord, maker of heaven and earth, bless you from Zion.
>
> Psalm 134:3 Tanakh Translation

Gathering for an all-night Bible study is not the way most kids would choose to celebrate a big holiday. It certainly doesn't have the same appeal as, say, eating giant wedges of cheesecake, parading around with fruit on a stick, or festooning the whole place with plants and flowers. But all of these are age-old traditions for celebrating Shavuot, the harvesttime Feast of Weeks.[152] Of course, you don't have to eat cheesecake. Anything dairy-forward or honey-laden will do. It's one of the ways we taste and celebrate the bounty of ancient Israel, that place flowing with milk and honey. This most popular custom is a spiritual excuse to load up on blintzes, quiche, or a sprawling cheese board. Or just a generous bowl of ice cream!

Growing up, I couldn't wait for those homemade crepes to slide off Mom's yellow pan, perfectly delicate and warm. My sister and I would fold them around the traditional sweet and tangy blend of cream cheese and cottage cheese and then top them with fresh or syrupy fruit. I would have eaten those blintzes for every meal if given the choice. Those little cheesecake wraps are absolute bliss—especially now, when coupled with my sweet childhood memories. Blissful blintzes.

What wasn't so blissful was my nostalgic attempt to whip up my grandmother's recipe for cheese pancakes. That mixture of cottage cheese, flour, cinnamon, and sugar resulted in a mess of molten goo that found its way into every single crevice of my new stovetop. Sometimes I think it's safer for me to keep things simple and just serve a goat cheese salad. Which, to be fair, is pretty authentic, since goats were the main source of milk in the Promised Land.[153]

Whichever of these Shavuot traditions we embrace in these diaspora days, we set aside time to delight in the flourishing of the Promised Land and to offer thanks for God's provision in our own lives. In case I haven't stressed it enough, food takes center stage in virtually every Jewish feast and festival. We take our cues from God's commands and from the purpose of each holiday. There are the fruits and veggies decorating our makeshift huts for the Feast of Booths. There is the unleavened bread and the bitter herbs on Passover's table. And for the Feast of Weeks—also known as the Feast of Firstfruits—we curate menus featuring the ancient crops of the Holy Land. Back when the Temple stood, the nation brought freewill offerings from all of this bounty to Jerusalem—fresh, if they lived nearby, or dried, if they had to travel a great distance.[154] Gathered together at the sanctuary, Israel offered thanks for the bounty of Canaan, that sliver of a nation "flowing with milk and honey" (Exod. 3:8; Num. 14:8; Deut. 31:20 NIV).

That "milk and honey" phrase God so often used to describe the Promised Land was a common, proverbial expression at the time. It captured the fertility of lands in the Middle East, conjuring up visions of lush orchards, golden harvests, and countless cattle on a thousand hills.[155] If you've ever visited the Holy Land, you may be raising an eyebrow in skepticism. I admit that, with few exceptions, the Land of promise may not look too promising from an agricultural perspective. Outside of the fertile valleys, the landscape is mostly arid and rocky unless it has been masterfully irrigated, as much of modern Israel is. But archaeological evidence points to a region that was far more fertile than it is today, and ancient texts paint a picture of rich forests and fields covering the entire land of Canaan.[156] Egyptian scribes marveled at Israel's wealth of wine, honey, and olives and at the abundance of bread, wine, meat, and milk that filled the nation's dinner plates on a daily basis.[157]

That lush terrain is what God offered to the downtrodden house of Jacob. From the burning bush to the brink of the Jordan River, God assured His people that the homeland He had for them was oozing with the proverbial milk and honey. Twelve of the Israelites had actually seen this fertility with their very own eyes. Led by Caleb and Joshua, this team returned from Canaan bearing a single cluster of grapes so massive that it required two of them to carry it—not to mention a cache of pomegranates and figs (Num. 13:23). Unfortunately, despite this irrefutable evidence of God's trustworthiness, the ten other scouts doubted the rest of God's vow that He would settle Israel back in the Land promised to Abraham, Isaac, and Jacob (Gen. 12:7; 15:18; 26:3; 28:13–15). Instead, they focused on Canaan's towering residents, insisting that the Land would devour them all (Num. 13:31–33). These ten convinced all the Israelites to join them in their doubts and fears (Num. 13:22–14:4).

I am sometimes tempted to berate this stubborn bunch. But I realize that I, too, am constantly thanking God for His goodness in one breath and then doubting Him with the next. The Israelites were also still recovering from the trauma born from generations of oppression under Pharaoh followed by their harrowing escape. A little grace is due them. The grace that God gave them for their mistrust was forty years of meandering Egypt's wasteland—one year for each day of the scouting mission. Even though it seems like a punishment, it could also be viewed as a gift. Those years adrift provided an abundance of time to learn how to trust God in every circumstance. He certainly never withdrew His promises of permanence and fertility, and He never abandoned them during their journey.

At long last, after Israel's generation-long wandering, the nation finally stood at the edge of the Promised Land. Their hearts must have skipped at the thought of finally leaving the barren desert and entering the Land dripping with fertility. Their mouths must have watered in anticipation of milk and honey and those legendary grapes. From barley and wheat, Israel would be able to bake bread and cake. From grapes and olives, they would press wine and oil. From dates and figs, they would prepare honey and jam. And instead of only decorative pomegranates hanging from the high priest's hem, real fruit bursting with scarlet juice and seeds would fill the trees (Exod. 28:33–34). Hills and pastures would teem with sheep and goats, providing an endless supply of milk, meat, and wool. Israel would finally—after centuries in Egypt and decades in the desert—reclaim their ancestral roots in both location and profession. The Hebrews were at last returning to the Land where the flocks of Abraham, Isaac, and Jacob had multiplied and flourished.

After the Israelites finally crossed over the River Jordan—through another supernatural rolling back of water—God's rescued people celebrated their first Passover in the Promised Land (Josh. 5:10). The good news of their deliverance from Egypt was felt more deeply as they reclined on Canaan's soil and deeper still as they remembered Moses, the one who had shepherded them through the whole journey. God Himself had buried Moses somewhere in the valley of Moab before they made the final push to Canaan's border (Deut. 34:5–6). The grieving Israelites were now left to forge their new identity as they entered the Land.

Punctuating the transition to this new era, the daily manna—their divine daily sustenance for forty years—ended once they pushed back from that first Passover meal in Canaan, never to resume again (Josh. 5:10–12). It was time. God knew the people were ready. They marked the occasion most appropriately with unleavened bread and roasted grain plucked from the Promised Land. The days of wilderness wandering were over. They would begin to eat by the work of their hands and the sweat of their brow. And this meant that the Feast of Weeks would no longer be a theoretical exercise but a practical reality. Once again, a promise couched in a command was blossoming. The people's ability to offer up their firstfruits would now take root along with their crops.

> None shall appear before me empty-handed. You shall keep the Feast of [Weeks], of the firstfruits of your labor, of what you sow in the field.
>
> (Exod. 23:15b–16a ESV)

> For you will count up to the day after the seventh week, which day is the fiftieth; then you will offer the first cereal-offering from the new wheat crop to the Eternal. You will bring from wheat grown in the Land of Israel two loaves for waving, each made of two-tenths of an epha of fine flour, baked leavened, a first-fruit offering to the Eternal.
>
> (Lev. 23:16–17 Torah Yesharah)

In the Promised Land, God's rescued people had been replanted. They could begin to cultivate fields and orchards from which to live. With each passing year, the Land yielded increasing bounty. And so, with each passing year, the nation's annual offerings of firstfruits increased in kind. At each summer's end, all of Israel carted their troves of offerings to the sanctuary for the Feast of Weeks. There they would celebrate God's goodness together. They brought their firstfruits not only of the wheat fields, but of every crop, from grain to fruits to bits of wool (Deut. 18:4).[158] These personal offerings overflowed in a tangible form of gratefulness to the Creator of the land, sun, and rain who had caused it all to grow.

Once everyone offered their first yield at the sanctuary, God's blessing would settle on all the rest of Israel's harvest. People were free then to use and to trade as they saw fit. This annual cycle of planting and harvesting and offering cultivated hearts marked by trust and gratitude. And within this annual cycle, God tied a knot between the Feast of Weeks and the Feast of Passover. In the spring, they had offered the first sheaves of barley—the *first* grain crop to ripen—from that field down in the Kidron Valley during Passover. Now, on the Feast of Weeks, they were to offer the first sheaves of wheat, the last grain to ripen. These spring and summer pilgrimage feasts formed the bookends of Israel's harvest, bracketing the season of growth that burgeoned during the seven weeks between them.

The growing between the two first reapings of grain took place not only in the farmers' fields but also in the nature of the wave offerings themselves. God's prescribed barley offering, you may remember, was to be made from one tenth of an ephah, without leavening, and offered as raw dough on the altar. In many ways it seemed like a moment of secondary importance, overshadowed by Passover's sacrifices and celebration of redemption. In contrast, the Feast of Weeks wheat offering stood front and center as the hallmark moment of that pilgrimage feast. Its wave offering was made from twice the amount of flour, leavened, and then waved in the form of two oversized, baked loaves. The visual differences between the two offerings were dramatic. From small to large, flat to risen, unfinished to finished, and sideshow to center stage, the Feast of Weeks offering paralleled what had been happening across the nation's fields. The two risen loaves waving through the air were a sort of grand finale for the entire agricultural season.

Yet this crescendo between Passover and the Feast of Weeks is about so much more than the rhythm of sowing and reaping. These pilgrimage bookends and the counting of the days between them have everything to do with God's relationship with His people. And it is all tied up in the specific day on which God said to celebrate the Feast of Weeks. Now, to clarify, God didn't assign a specific, independent date to this feast like He did for the others. Instead, He fixed its timing in a way that would keep it permanently attached to Passover.

> You will start to count from the night after the first day of the Passover holiday, from the day you bring the Omer that is waved: Seven complete weeks will there be, for you will count up to the day after the seventh week, which day is the fiftieth; then you will offer the first cereal-offering from the new wheat crop to the Eternal.
>
> (Lev. 23:15–16 Torah Yesharah)

When the Israelites received those instructions, they were encamped at the base of Mount Sinai. Every one of them knew exactly what had happened on the fiftieth day after God had delivered them out of Egypt. They knew, because it had just happened. It was as vivid and crisp in their collective memory as the blood on their doorposts and the splitting of the Red Sea. Closing their eyes, every single Israelite could see and hear and smell and feel everything that had happened to them on that fiftieth day. They would never forget that one singular moment anchoring them and all of Judaism to the desert mountain of Sinai.

Israel's fiftieth day as rescued refugees was the day of thunder and lightning on the mountain. It was the day on which all of Jacob's descendants assembled and trembled there at the foot of Mount Sinai. It was the day when God made good on His final Passover promise not only to rescue the Israelites but to draw them close as His very own people (Exod. 6:6–7). What happened on the fiftieth day completed Passover's redemption in dramatic fashion:

> Moses led the people out of the camp toward God, and they took their places at the foot of the mountain. Now Mount Sinai was all in smoke, for the LORD had come down upon it in fire; the smoke rose like the smoke of a kiln, and the whole mountain trembled violently. The blare of the horn grew louder and louder. As Moses spoke, God answered him in thunder.
>
> (Exod. 19:17–19 JPS)

> You have seen what I did to the Egyptians, how I bore you on eagles' wings and brought you to Me. Now then, if you will obey Me faithfully and keep My covenant, you shall be My treasured possession among all the peoples. Indeed, all the earth is Mine, but you shall be to Me a kingdom of priests and a holy nation.
>
> (Exod. 19:4–6a JPS)

> The LORD said to Moses: Thus shall you say to the Israelites: You yourselves saw that I spoke to you from the very heavens.
>
> (Exod. 20:19 JPS)

In the midst of Israel's Egyptian despair, God had courted them with the extravagant gift of freedom, and He didn't attach a single string. Then, fifty days after the rescue, they all gathered at the very same spot where God had first declared His intentions to Moses (Exod. 3:12).[159] Now, the great I AM thundered His vows to all of them through fire and smoke at the altar of Mount Sinai. A wedding-vow analogy may seem like a poetic stretch. But God has always likened His relationship with Israel to a marriage, a coupling set in motion at Passover and cemented with the everlasting covenant at Sinai. On that fiftieth day after freedom, the eternally faithful One pledged Himself to a people forever.

It was a ceremony like no other. Heaven literally sounded the trumpets, and the notes of the wedding march grew louder and louder as the Bridegroom approached (Exod. 19:16–19). Flames descended like attendants, surrounding Him at the altar. And the God of the universe shielded His bride with a veil of smoke, allowing Him to draw near to His treasure. He drew so near that Israel could hear His voice for the very first time and feel the heat of His breath with every word. Israel not only heard and felt His thundering voice but could actually *see* it.* The mountain shook under the weight of glory. Smoky air hung thick with holiness. The One who had just wielded all of nature against Egypt in their defense now harnessed His might and directed it in love toward His redeemed. It was a supernatural declaration of faithfulness and steadfast devotion. In the midst of that divine spectacle of fire and fume and thunderous reveille, God gave Himself to the people who had pledged their own devotion to Him: "All that Yahweh has spoken we will do!" (Exod. 19:8 LSB). And by the power vested through Himself, God pronounced them joined together:

> For your Maker is your bridegroom, his name, GOD-of-the-Angel-Armies! Your Redeemer is The Holy of Israel, known as God of the whole earth.
>
> (Isa. 54:5 MSG)

*Midrash Shemot Rabbah 5:9; Volli, *Cherubim*, 521–32. The ancient teaching, expanding on the literal Hebrew of Exodus 20, is that God's voice divided into seventy different voices—with seventy being symbolic of the nations of the earth. "And all the people saw the voices and the torches, the sound of the shofar, and the smoking mountain, and the people saw and trembled; so they stood from afar" (Exod. 20:15 CJB; Exod. 20:18 in Christian translations).

After hundreds of years living as oppressed foreigners, the people of Abraham, Isaac, and Jacob discovered that they were, in fact, the Almighty's treasure, regardless of their mortar-caked hands and tearstained faces. The only dowry God requested was fidelity. And Israel signed on the dotted line. That ancient marriage contract provided for a life of flourishing, harmony, and health. It explained how to honor and love the divine Bridegroom and how to honor and love one another as fellow members of the covenant. It also explained how to be restored to Him and to each other in the wake of our inevitable failings.

The spectacular marriage on the mountain marked the fulfillment of God's fourth and final Passover promise from Exodus 6. He had already delivered Jacob's descendants out of Egypt. He had freed them from Pharaoh's oppression. He had rescued every one of them with His mighty outstretched arm. Now, at last, God had drawn them close as His very own people. The Israelites now understood that, all along, God had not intended to simply free them *from* something but also *to* something—or, rather, to some*one:* Himself. This is the reason that the Feast of Weeks is considered the final day of Passover, forever coupled to the redemption from Egypt. From that day forward, throughout the honeymoon of the wilderness, God's guiding pillar of cloud and fire would be a dramatic, ever-present reminder of the moment when heaven met earth on their "first" fiftieth day.

That otherworldly marriage ceremony remains the bedrock of Judaism's union with God, thousands of years later. And by using that wedding day as the annual date for Israel to pilgrimage to the sanctuary with their firstfruits, God created a beautiful way to celebrate this anniversary. Once settled in the Promised Land, all of Israel would pilgrimage from far and wide to gather at His earthly home, their arms overflowing with the very bounty He had promised. Each annual offering of firstfruits became a lavish anniversary gift to the One who had called them, freed them, and wed them to Himself. By God's design, the counting of days between Passover and the Feast of Weeks created a season of growing anticipation. Everyone's eyes fixed collectively on that remarkable fiftieth day.

Even now, dispersed throughout the world and without the Temple to draw us together, Jews still begin anticipating the Sinai anniversary at the beginning of Passover. We recount the ancient waving of the first bit of harvested barley and then we start counting just like our ancestors did. Like them, we don't count down from Passover's barley sheaf, we count up. *Day one of the counting of the omer, day two of the counting of the omer, day three of the counting of the omer*. And so on, until the fiftieth day. As the numbers grow, so does our anticipation—like a bride stepping closer and closer to the altar. During these fifty days, our gratefulness grows from the symbolic poverty of the Passover bread to the wealth of covenant bread: unleavened to leavened, unfinished to finished, brittle to bountiful. Our spirits swell with increasing lightness at the thought of celebrating who we are, the beloved of God. Even our nickname for the Feast of Weeks—*Chag ha'Azereth*, the "Feast of Conclusion"—captures the way Passover and Shavuot are bound together. Even though our hearts ache over the absence of the Temple, pillaged and reduced to rubble by Rome, we choose to rejoice in the steadfast love of the God who still invites us to draw near.

Like our pilgrimaging ancestors, we count the days between the two feasts like the delicate links on a chain of gold. We count them in the synagogue, in our homes, and on our phones (yes, there's an app for that). On the fiftieth day, we listen to Exodus 19 and 20 while worshiping in the synagogue, together reciting the Ten Commandments. In doing so, we rejoice in the fact that He loves us, and we remember that He still cares deeply about our posture toward Him and toward our neighbors. We decorate our homes and sanctuaries with plants and blooms to celebrate the Tree of Life that is God's word and to remember our ancestors' offerings of bounty.[160] And though we are no longer able to make a pilgrimage to His altar, we still celebrate God's goodness by striving to give Him the firstfruits of our hearts, minds, lives, and loves.

We also celebrate by eating blintzes. I openly confess that I have never stayed awake all night studying Scripture to welcome this holy anniversary, nor have I personally decorated our home with ferns and flowers—although this confession is inspiring me to start. I do, however, eat lots of blintzes, cheesecake, and creme brulé. Each morsel calls to mind God's ancient promises of milk and honey—promises made and kept. Each dish prompts me to imagine the richness that flowed throughout the Land and then into the baskets carried up to Jerusalem. Every crumb and drop stirs gratefulness in my heart for the faithful words of God—spiritual milk and honey that nourish and sweeten this life.

All of these things help me remember in that ancient way of remembering, just like Jerusalem's pilgrims did. We remember as people who were there. On Passover, we remember as ones who were there in Egypt, placing ourselves under the covering blood of the lambs. And on the Feast of Weeks, we remember as if we, too, stood at the foot of the mountain on that fiftieth day, placing ourselves under the veil of Sinai's smoke.

Mount Sinai still stands as an ancient witness, the grandest of all Ebenezer stones. On that peak, the great I AM first spoke to Moses through supernatural flames. It was there that God made His promise to rescue the limping children of Abraham and to then carry them back to that same holy ground, soon and very soon. In just a matter of months, He made good on that seemingly impossible pledge. The Creator shook the mountain to its core through fire, smoke, and thunder, marrying heaven and earth in a covenant of steadfast love. Mount Sinai forever testifies to the powerful and steadfast love of our God. And it testifies that He will move mountains to draw us near.

I think about God's voice reaching the ears of all the Israelites that day for the very first time. And I also think about His voice reaching my own ears, revealing Himself in ways I had never imagined. In all these generations between us, the word and the heart of God have not changed. In the desert, God made Himself known to my ancestors, a nation of wounded, broken, empty-handed people. Today, He still makes Himself known to us—people who are just as wounded, broken, and empty-handed as they were. As it was for the Israelites, God's revelation of who He is and how He loves us anchors my life, whether I'm living through a season of desert wandering or flourishing harvest.

That fiftieth day is an anniversary like no other. It speaks of power, love, and grateful hearts. These days, when I reflect on the ancient wheat offering, I give thanks that God's Word is bread. I give thanks that the Messiah Himself is eternal manna, the daily Bread of Life that sustains in just the right way at just the right time. I am reminded that Passover's bread of affliction eventually gives way to the Feast of Weeks risen loaves. And I am overcome by the knowledge that our lives, which are currently marked by death, will ultimately be marked by eternal light. Remembering all these things on the fiftieth day, I bless wine and candles and bread and brulé, offering up the firstfruits of my heart to the Bridegroom of Heaven, the forever faithful One abounding in love.

Jerusalem calls us to covenant.

CHAPTER 11

Waving Wheat

O Israel, wait for the LORD; for with the LORD is steadfast love and great power to redeem.

Psalm 130:7 JPS85

The walls of our mid-century modern home boast many pieces of my grandmother's art. Grandma Marion earned her Master of Fine Arts from Columbia University and did her doctoral work at New York University. As a female college professor in the 1960s and 1970s, Marion Scheibel was a wonder. Her paintings, sculptures, and wood-block prints graced local galleries and family homes. She created greeting cards for synagogues and posters for her university. Grandma even designed the small cottage on Lagoon Pond where she and Grandpa Jud lived in the summers, built on the bones of a tiny, rustic cabin. Grandma's great love of art and architecture was evident in her weekly field trips with her New Jersey college students to The Metropolitan Museum of Art, or—as she called it—her "off-campus classroom."[161]

At five-foot-two, Grandma Marion was a spitfire, easily making up for the height differential between her and Grandpa Jud, who towered over her. Pictures of them together are a delight. And, as beautifully as she could carve clay and layer oils, Marion could also scale a fish and bake a pie with a skill that I've yet to match. She directed my sister and me around the kitchen as if we were her students. And we were. No matter what we cooked up, it tasted better because we had made it together.

Whether she was creating art, teaching students, preparing Thanksgiving, or dancing the Charleston with Grandpa Jud in competitions at the synagogue, Grandma Marion's energy always surpassed even my childhood supply. I treasured our two-mile walks followed by lagoon swims on early summer mornings. We wrapped up those outings with bowls of yogurt topped with farm-stand berries and drizzled with local honey. We two early risers usually accomplished all of this before anyone else woke up. By the time the rest of the crew shuffled to the breakfast table, Grandma was already packing lunches for a day at the shore, where she would *not* snooze in the sun. Instead, she would walk beyond the tide and swim back and forth, parallel to the shoreline, wearing her white swim cap covered in floppy petals. From my sleepy view in an old beach chair, Grandma looked like a bridal bouquet, bobbing along with the tide for what seemed like hours. Marion Ruth was buoyant, in every sense of the word.

I think about her every day. She and all of my grandparents smile at me from picture frames in my bedroom. But I especially miss Grandma on Shavuot, the Feast of Weeks. Since as early as AD 600, the traditional text read in synagogue on the morning of the feast is the book of Ruth.[162] So I get a bit misty sometimes when I listen to that ancient narrative, missing my Marion Ruth, a woman just as industrious and fierce in spirit as King David's great-grandmother.

The author of this *megilla*, this scroll, is said to be none other than the prophet Samuel.[163] And with simple time stamps at the end of the first two chapters, he captures one of the two reasons why we read Ruth's story during the Feast of Weeks. In the last verse of Ruth 1, Samuel writes, without any elaboration, that Ruth and Naomi—a young Moabite widow and her widowed mother-in-law—arrived in Bethlehem at the beginning of the barley harvest (Ruth 1:22). In the same way, in the last verse of Ruth 2, Samuel writes that Ruth gleaned in the fields until the end of the wheat harvest (Ruth 2:23). Based on what we know about the timing of the two grain harvests, these seemingly unremarkable verses actually add great depth to the story. They tell us that Naomi and Ruth arrived in Bethlehem either during or immediately after Passover, and that Ruth gleaned leftovers from the fields until just after the Feast of Weeks.

The thought of two vulnerable widows arriving together in the breadbasket of Israel at the beginning of the barley harvest is incredibly moving to me.[164] They were stepping into the Promised Land right as the whole nation was celebrating their rescue from Pharoah's oppression. God's people had just witnessed the priest wave the barley offering before the altar and throw the handful of dough on the fire. And now they were all counting toward the wheat harvest and the fiftieth day. The seven-week season of grain growing and harvesting was fully underway.

Hungry and empty-handed, Ruth set out to see if God's people would really do what He had commanded: Leave the edges of their fields and vineyards unharvested so that the poor and the foreigner can gather food (Lev. 23:22). Ruth found that they, in fact, did—including Boaz, the son of Rahab. Maybe Boaz remembered how his own gentile mother had been marginalized before she married into the clan of Judah. Or maybe Boaz was simply a kind person who sought to follow God's commands, even toward the least of these. Whatever Boaz's reasons, Ruth's personal harvest of grain—and of love—grew exponentially during those summer days between Passover and the Feast of Weeks. As the omer count grew closer and closer to the fiftieth day, Ruth's sense of security and belonging grew as well.

I've always been curious about whether Ruth traveled the twenty-five miles north to celebrate the Feast of Weeks in Shiloh during her first summer in Israel. Perhaps she worked as a servant, carrying firstfruits to the tabernacle after helping to prepare the offerings in Bethlehem.[165] Or maybe she went as part of the festal throng, offering thanks to God for the gleanings that He had provided for her and Naomi.[166] Ruth was certainly welcome to take part in the celebration, since God made it clear that Israel was to include sons and daughters, servants and Levites, foreigners and orphans, and even the widows living among them (Deut. 16:10–11). Ruth definitely checked more than one box on God's guest list.

I would like to think that people in Bethlehem encouraged Ruth to take part in the pilgrimage that summer. But whether or not she made the trip, I wonder what she thought about Israel's covenant celebration. Ruth was, after all, a foreign widow who had chosen to say "I do" to Israel's Covenant-Maker. Most people recognize her famous declaration to her Israelite mother-in-law, even if they don't know where it came from: "For wherever you go, I will go; wherever you lodge, I will lodge; your people shall be my people, and your God my God" (Ruth 1:16 JPS).

Even if Ruth didn't travel to Shiloh that summer to celebrate the Sinai anniversary and dedicate the nation's firstfruits, the Moabite had pledged herself to the God of Israel. Despite Naomi's urging for Ruth to return to Moab—where she could start a new life rather than share in her mother-in-law's grief and widowhood in Judah—Ruth would not be dissuaded (Ruth 1:6–17). She voluntarily and unwaveringly bound herself to Yahweh. Ruth's determination to be grafted into the covenant is the other reason why we read her story during the Feast of Weeks. She willingly embraced Adonai and His Torah, just as Naomi's forebears had done at Mount Sinai.[167] Soon, Ruth also covenanted herself to Boaz. The family line of these two compassionate souls would grow and blossom to include their great-grandson King David, as well as all of the messianic promises God would assign to David's throne (Ruth 4:18–22; Matt. 1:1–17).

The book of Ruth is just four short chapters, yet I find it to be one of the most powerful accounts in Scripture. The narrative of her first Bethlehem summer is a beautiful testimony of the ways that God guides and abides in the middle of feast and famine. Everything that unfolded around Ruth, Naomi, and Boaz speaks so loudly of God's care and concern for the vulnerable. Their story celebrates strangers outside of the covenant becoming part of the family. And it showcases God's fantastic habit of weaving together unlikely lives in order to bring about redemption. During that single season of harvest in Bethlehem, God redeemed Ruth's personal heartache and, in doing so, stitched together a significant part of His redemption plan. Her story is truly something to behold.

Meanwhile, oblivious to the messianic tapestry being woven among them during the eleventh century BC, the rest of Israel went about tending their fields and orchards just like they did every year. The forty-nine days between Passover and Shavuot were so critical to the success of the nation's harvest. Without the right balance of sun and rain and of north and south winds, their primary crops would not ripen well.[168] And so, after witnessing the waving of the barley offering at the sanctuary, the Passover pilgrims returned home to care for their own crops. In the growing warmth of spring, every household began to identify the first sheaves and buds emerging from every variety of growth. "These are the firstfruits!" God's people proclaimed as they tied scarlet threads around the blossoming firstfruits.[169] Marking the gifts they would nurture and give back to the Lord was treated as an occasion for rejoicing.

By midsummer, when the counting of the omer neared its crescendo, all of Israel would set out with scythe, hook, and basket. Each household gathered the first and best from every scarlet-tied stem of the fields, orchards, and vines. They carefully packed these offerings in baskets of gold, silver, palm leaves, or straw, depending on their means.[170] Firstfruits that would spoil before the fiftieth day were dried, if possible, or sold and the proceeds added to the family's offering baskets.[171] Finally, when it was time to leave for Jerusalem's sanctuary, the pilgrims would set off with bounty balanced on heads and loaded on oxen. Even those beasts of burden were bedecked for the occasion, with their heads crowned by olive branches and their horns covered in gold.[172] Even families running late for the feast still took the time to gild their oxen's horns, except the latecomers used silver instead of gold.[173] Firstfruits of the flocks and herds—even something as small as a dove—often trailed behind the pilgrims. Everyone had something to bring to Jerusalem.

Along the roadway, the summer sun glinted off the baskets in the pilgrims' arms, and songs of praise rose into the air. In the days of the Temple, paths and roads merged on all sides of Jerusalem. At crossroads in places like Bethel, Hebron, and Jericho, the masses of people and baskets and animals would swell in their final ascent. This harvest parade must have been something to behold—both for those traveling within it and for the people watching from afar. Each step brought them closer to adding their own firstfruits to the cornucopia spilling over on Mount Zion. Along the roadway, they played flutes and sang from Psalm 122: "I was happy when they said to me, let us go to the house of the Lord!"[174] At last, on the day before the feast, pilgrims converged on the holy city with their gifts.[175]

Whether royal, lowly, or somewhere in between, each household readied its offerings with as much finery as possible.

Seven-tiered basket towers abounded, looking like vertical cornucopia filling the sanctuary complex.[176] Each tier held firstfruits from one of the seven species of the Promised Land: barley, wheat, olives, dates, pomegranates, grapes, and figs. They ascended from the largest basket on the bottom—filled to the brim with inexpensive barley—all the way up to the smallest, crowning basket of juicy figs, having just been brought to perfect ripeness by the midsummer sun. Some pilgrims even went a step further, topping the whole thing off with a live dove tethered to an additional, eighth tier.[177] Even Israel's kings brought their personal offerings right alongside the citizenry, entering through the Hulda Gate with baskets of fruit and grain on their shoulders.[178] Every year, the circle of God's provision found its completion there, at His dwelling place, as grain and fruit, wool and milk made their way back to their source—the Creator and Provider of all.

In the midst of the joyful, pre-feast melee, the Levites eventually sounded the trumpets from the Temple Mount. The Feast of Weeks, with its dramatic wave offering, was about to commence. Priests readied the two risen loaves of wheat and the twenty-four animals that God had specified for the festal sacrifice.[179] As they worked, the soft melody of a single flute accompanied the Levites' joyous song, drawing the sea of pilgrims to the courtyard. The growing congregation repeated lyrics responsively, anticipating the celebrated waving of the bread of firstfruits (Lev. 23:20).[180]

Those two loaves were a sight to behold. So much care had gone into them. Priests had winnowed all the wheat kernels for the offering by hand just a day or two earlier.[181] They had rubbed the grains with their fingers three hundred times and struck them with their fists and their palms five hundred times, until every bit of chaff and fiber had fallen away.[182] Then, after winnowing and grinding the kernels with the millstone, the priests passed the flour through a succession of twelve finer and finer sieves, producing two-tenths of an ephah of the purest, finest flour.

On the evening of the forty-ninth day, the priests divided the flour in half and separately prepared two batches of leavened dough.[183] The two loaves, also baked separately, were enormous in size and unusual in shape. Each one measured seven handbreadths long, four handbreadths wide, and four fingers high. The baking priests fashioned hornlike protrusions that extended from the four corners of each loaf.[184] Perhaps the striking shape was a nod to the horns on the sacrificial altar.

With music filling the air, the ritual began. A single priest took the two loaves from their special tray, and placed them on top of the two live, peace-offering lambs, raising them high in the air (Lev. 23:20).[185] This feat of lifting and waving two live lambs and two large loaves is difficult to envision. Yet every year they did it somehow, and then did it a second time. For the second waving—conducted after all of the animal sacrifices—the loaves were coupled with the breast and right hind leg of the now-sacrificed peace-offering lambs.[186] North and south, east and west, up and down, the priests waved the offering of bread and lamb, just as all of Israel had done with their bundled greenery during the Feast of Booths and as the priest had done with the barley offering at Passover. Again and again, from season to season, the community affirmed that everything belongs to God and that His faithful presence is everywhere.

God's presence was felt not only there at the altar but also in the Chamber of the Hearth, built within the north wall of the courtyard, by the Gate of the Offering.[187] Normally used as sleeping quarters for the priestly watch on duty, the large room now served as a quiet haven for the priests who had just conducted the wave and burnt offerings. Assembling under its domed ceiling, they sat together along rows of stone benches that extended from the walls.[188] Two of their company entered the darkened chamber, bearing one of the loaves and one of the lambs, the rest having already been set aside for the high priest's family (Lev. 23:20; Num. 18:12).[189]

Each one of these assembled sons of Aaron received only a morsel of bread and lamb once it was divided among them all. Yet even the smallest taste of this "holiest of the holy" offerings was considered a treasure.[190] The priests would savor this moment together not only because of the sacred nature of their tiny feast but also because they knew that the quiet, coolness, and rest would not last. It would soon be time for the multitude of pilgrims to offer their individual gifts.

Enveloped by the aroma of grain and peace offerings, the worshipers were ready to offer their own firstfruits: all those gilded baskets of bounty carried to Jerusalem as anniversary gifts to God on that fiftieth day. The gates of the Temple courtyard had been thrown open at midnight the night before so that the first shift of priests could inspect all the animals brought as offerings.[191] There were, in fact, so many offerings brought to the sanctuary that, even though the feast technically lasted only one day, it took up to a full week for every pilgrim household to offer their gifts.[192]

Whatever the system for receiving the offerings happened to be—whether by tribe, place of residence, or first come, first served—a representative from each family would eventually stand before one of the priests with their gifts balanced upon one shoulder. Never had people from the greatest to the least been so happy to give away their very best. The Temple courtyard filled with the beautiful, buzzing din of countless worshipers reciting Deuteronomy 26:5–9. It was God's prescribed monologue for each offeror, a recounting of Israel's history from the days of Abraham's wandering to the sorrow of Egypt's oppression to the fruitfulness found in the Land of milk and honey (Deut. 26:5–10). Standing before the magnificent Temple, free in their own land, this collective retelling would ensure that Israel always remembered how they had been loved by the God of heaven. That repeated refrain of Deuteronomy's remembrance filled the midsummer air, day in and day out, until the very last gift was given.

After reciting the Deuteronomy passage, each offeror would lower their offerings to the ground at the feet of the priest who stood with him. The priests lifted the pilgrims' baskets up from the ground and waved their firstfruits (as you can imagine) north, south, east, west, up, and down.[193] Finally, with empty hands and glad hearts, each offeror made their way toward the courtyard gates. Before exiting the sanctuary courts, though, they each stopped to lay prostrate on the ground in one last act of worship and thanksgiving.[194] Face down and shoulder to shoulder at the dwelling place of God, hundreds of thousands of pilgrims worshiped in that living, breathing blanket of devotion on the Temple Mount, just like King David had urged Israel to do: "Let us go and sing to the Lord. . . . Come, let us prostate ourselves and bow; let us kneel before the L rd who made us" (Ps. 95:1, 6).*

Each day that the offerings continued, the baskets of plenty made their way to the Chamber of the Hearth, where the ministering priests rested between their courtyard shifts. The sheer number of them required to receive and wave every gift that week must have been staggering. Inside the quiet, domed chamber, the priests rested and were nourished by all those gifts of gratitude (Num. 18:13; Ezek. 44:30).[195] They tasted and saw that they, too—though they had no crops or land to call their own—were nourished and sustained by God's provision through the Land.

Between the loaves of the nation, the aroma of the peace offerings, and the gifts of prostrate people, the Feast of Weeks was marked by unity in gratitude, worship, and joy. In fact, the

*From Psalm 95, the Rashi Ketuvim version. The space in "L rd" is intentional. Because of the holiness of God's self-proclaimed name and the prohibition against saying it out loud, even written translations are not typically spelled out completely.

days after the official feast day eventually became known as *Isru Hag*, meaning "bind [the] festival." It comes from Psalm 118, a Hallel psalm that speaks of binding the festival offering to the altar. During the extra days it took for everyone to present their firstfruits, the whole nation seemed to linger. The pilgrims chose to bind themselves to Jerusalem and to one another, even after their own firstfruits had been offered up. It allowed them to hold onto the rejoicing for just a little while longer.

I love the joy of this image. I love picturing the pilgrims' determination to bring their first and best to God. I love picturing ancient priests using their hands to winnow wheat and bake bread. And I love imagining hundreds of thousands of worshipers recounting Israel's history together in the shadow of the Temple. It is moving to envision God's ministers treasuring even the smallest morsels of His holiest offerings. And it captivates my heart to think about my people clinging to fruit-filled days of joy in Jerusalem and not letting go, of wanting to remain together for just a little while longer.

These images remind me of my own treasured memories, remembrances of my own family coming together from around the nation to share gratitude around a table of bounty every year in modern-day America. I love Thanksgiving memories of family reunions around crowded tables. Whether we gathered in the frigid cold of Iowa, Wisconsin, or New Jersey or in the warmth of Florida or California, it was always so hard to let the feast go. That fullness of love, laughter, and movie marathons always returns when I remember those usually blustery November days.

I still make Grandma Marion's bread stuffing every Thanksgiving, using the now spice-smudged envelope on which I had scribbled her instructions. I remember exactly where I stood in my tiny Nashville kitchen when I grabbed that scrap from the crumb-covered counter. Even my body remembers the stress of that motherhood moment: unearthing a dull pencil from the junk drawer, cradling the cordless phone between my ear and shoulder, trying to soothe my colicky baby and my hungry toddler, all while listening to that cheerful voice coaching me from miles away. I wish I could go back to that now-nostalgic moment and hold on to each one of them just the way they were that day: my baby, my toddler, and my Marion Ruth. I wish I could hold on to them a little while longer, just like my ancestors chose to cling to each other in those ancient pilgrimage days.

But I also remember a different, achingly sad time and place when I did not want to let go of Marion Ruth. My aunt was waiting patiently, ready to whisk me to the airport so I could return to my loves back home. But I wasn't ready to let go of *this* love, my grandma. I couldn't let go of the woman who had infused color and light into so many lives. And so I clung to her, and she to me, wedged together on her hospital bed amid beeps and whirs and the smell of disinfectant. I hate cancer, by the way. During those few days, I had grown accustomed to the yellow of her skin. But the shock of her shoulder blades through the thin hospital gown caught me off guard in that moment. I remember my eyes streaming and my breath catching.

Then her soft words filled my ear: "Tam, I just wish you hadn't left our people." I pulled back just a few inches, each of our searching blue eyes holding the other's. "Oh, Grandma," I whispered back, both of us still holding on. "I didn't leave. I just found the Jewish Messiah." We smiled through our tears and returned to our embrace. I will always treasure the unfiltered honesty and love of those moments. I only wish we hadn't waited until the end to express them.

Her laughter and wit still break into my thoughts, especially when I stop in front of her paintings where they hang at the front door, at the dinner table, over the mantel, between my children's bedrooms, and even in my little laundry room. She breaks into my thoughts when I read the book of Ruth, too. My sensory memories of Marion sometimes mingle with Scripture in a way that seems to animate Ruth, lifting her off the pages. Sometimes I find myself wondering about Ruth's relationship with her great-grandson. Did she and little David know one another—he, the youngest of Jesse's eight boys? Did he watch her hands deftly prepare bread from wheat still grown in the family fields the way I used to watch Grandma peel an entire apple in a single, unbroken spiral? Or was the love story of Ruth and Boaz the stuff of family legend by then? Whether or not David and Ruth ever shared sweet moments together, the king's life and line became forever entwined with the wheat fields of Bethlehem—from his own birth until the birth of his descendant, the promised Messiah, right there in that same small town, just as Micah had foretold (Mic. 5:2; Matt. 2:4–6).[196]

Now, thousands of years later, my people read about the life of Ruth every year on the anniversary of our covenant with God. We remember the fiftieth day by celebrating a gentile woman who joined the Jewish fold, a woman whose family tree birthed Israel's greatest king and the promised Messiah. Ruth's story reminds us that even in the bloodline of the Jewish Messiah, there are drops of gentile blood. And through her life, we commemorate the bounty of the Promised Land along with a foreshadowing of the Messiah's mission. Ruth had been grafted into God's chosen nation in the same way that her second mother-in-law, Rahab, had been. And one day, the Son of David would make a way for all of humanity to be grafted into the growing vine of His covenant people (Rom. 11:17).

Jerusalem calls us to harvest.

CHAPTER 12

Counting Up

The Lord will do great things for us and we shall rejoice.
Psalm 126:3 Tanakh Translation

With a suddenness that robbed us of goodbyes, my other grandma, Arliene, died on a Friday in November. Months later, my father handed me a wooden jewelry box. An inlay of flowers in muted pinks and yellows adorned the lid. He had discovered it while going through my grandparents' house in the days after the funeral, and he had tucked it away for me. Several more months passed before I could bring myself to open it. I ran my fingers across the red felt that lined the inside, discovering a flap at the bottom edge. That's when I realized that it was, in fact, a music box. I turned the winding key underneath and, despite its tarnished prongs, the mechanism still played "Lara's Theme" from *Dr. Zhivago* without a hitch. This gift seemed right to me, since Grandma Arliene had brought so much song to my life.

The musical jewelry box no longer held any jewelry, but that didn't surprise me. Besides, Grandma had already given me two necklaces that meant so much to both of us. One was the sparkling mezuzah pendant that my grandfather bought her during our bat mitzvah pilgrimage together.* The other was a pearl choker nestled inside a black velvet box. She had asked a jeweler to divide a long strand that my father bought for her during his draft tour in Vietnam when I was a baby. Eventually, I would wear my half of the pearl necklace at my wedding, carrying Grandma with me down the aisle in spirit even though she couldn't bring herself to come to the church ceremony. Those two very personal heirlooms bear the beauty of our relationship, conjuring up memories of faces and places so dear to me, then and now.

Grandma's music box was not completely empty, though. It held a never-opened bottle of Shalimar, still enclosed in its navy and gold-foil box. For more than a decade, I couldn't open it. But finally, in the days when I began writing this book, I fetched the wooden box from my bedroom closet, curled up on the sofa, and rested it in my lap. A few slow, determined notes of *Dr. Zhivago* escaped as I opened the lid and withdrew the glossy box. Carefully opening the flap, I slid the heavy glass bottle into my hand. I hesitated, but then slowly brought the nozzle up to my nose. I didn't even have to spray it. All these years later, in one of those beautiful scent-induced time warps, the tiniest of whiffs transported me back to childhood days sitting on her lap. It dropped me into the passenger seat of her Plymouth on morning drives to her print shop. It pulled me into her postage-stamp-sized kitchen, where I peeled eggs while listening to her stories. It nudged me toward the bathroom mirror where I watched her shadow her eyes and powder her nose. And

*A mezuzah is a small, decorative box that houses a scroll with the extended Shema prayer and passage. You'll see them on doorposts and on necklaces, taking seriously God's command to write His words on our doorposts. The scroll inside contains verses from Deuteronomy 6 and 11, reminding us to love the Lord our God with all our heart and soul and strength.

it wrapped me back up in her sometimes-too-tight embrace. My eyes are welling even now, just writing the words.

That's not to say that Grandma's perfume is the only scent that takes me back to her presence. There's also the smell of roses. That fragrance brings back memories of flowers in the hands of my grandpa, who stood on his front porch every Friday afternoon to present his bride with a Sabbath bouquet. There's the aroma of matzah ball soup simmering and fried chicken frying. And there's the smell of Grandma's tarnished Havdalah spice box—the one shaped like a turret—with its fragrant cinnamon stick tucked inside. Every so often, she would catch sight of me from the kitchen, gently lifting the filigreed tower from its spot on the corner shelf to take a whiff, and she would smile.

Havdalah—separation—is the ancient ritual of bidding farewell to the Sabbath, whether in our homes or in our synagogues. It's a warm and wonderful marker between Shabbat's rest and the new week's work. We bless the wine and pour it until the silver cup has literally runneth over onto a little saucer. It's a tangible depiction of the abundant joy found in our God. We breathe in the aroma of sweet spices, passing the box—or, in ancient days, a bouquet of myrrh—from hand to hand, drawing in the sweet fragrance of God's rest to sustain us during the week ahead. We bless and kindle a thick, braided candle, the flame reminding us of God's light, the braid reminding us of our unity in that light. Those flickering wicks dance to the tune of the last bit of liturgy, and then we dip the braid into the shimmering puddle of overflow, extinguishing the flames as the sun sets.

The Talmud teaches that, on one particular long-ago day, a heavenly fragrance filled the entire atmosphere, accompanying the breath of God's voice. On that fiftieth day of thunder and lightning on top of Mount Sinai, heaven's aroma flowed and filled every corner of the earth as God uttered each of the Ten Commandments.[197] Between each commandment, He swept the scent away with a great wind, allowing the world to be filled again and again in ten waves of divine aroma. Evidently, the fragrance of God's voice also served to rouse the Israelites, who—in their great fear and trembling—had become so overwhelmed at His majesty that they all collapsed in a nationwide fainting spell.[198] These poetic teachings eventually led to a tradition of scattering spice on the floors of homes and synagogues in celebration of the Feast of Weeks, the anniversary of that magnificent, fragrant, covenant-making day.

Perhaps, in later generations, pilgrims brought firstfruits from their spices along with their other gifts—if not for an offering, then at least to commemorate those fragrant waves of God's voice. Leading up to the feast, gardens throughout Israel swelled with sweetness as everyone counted the summer days to the feast. Every evening at sundown, from Passover to the fiftieth day, every single Jewish household in Israel and beyond blessed the Lord and then counted the day in that ritual called *Sefirat Ha-Omer*, the counting of the omer. *Today is day one of the omer. Today is day two of the omer.* After the first six days, the count also included the week: *Today is day ten, which is one week and three days of the omer.*[199]

Each and every twilight since returning home from the Passover feast in Jerusalem, God's people would count, just as He had said to do, and just as they had always done. The days and weeks following Jesus's final Passover—with all its horror, confusion, and rumors of rising—were no exception. That year, as the fiftieth day drew closer, the people's anticipation grew in greater measure than ever before, because instead of looking forward only to the bounty and joy of the feast in Jerusalem, the people of Judea wanted to see and hear what news there was of Jesus. Had He really risen out of the sealed garden tomb? Had there been fallout among the leaders over His crucifixion? Were Joseph and Nicodemus in trouble with the rest of the Sanhedrin? What did all of it mean? What did *any* of it mean? The only way to answer any of their questions was to return to Jerusalem for the Feast of Weeks.

Under normal circumstances, the Feast of Weeks didn't draw quite as many pilgrims as the Feasts of Tabernacles or Passover.[200] It wasn't out of the ordinary for people to occasionally send firstfruits along with extended family or friends if additional work in the fields made it difficult to go. But, whether from excitement or sheer curiosity, there were doubtless more pilgrims than usual that particular summer. The Passover multitudes would have wanted to return and be firsthand witnesses to whatever drama was still playing out around the Temple. But until the Feast of Weeks arrived, the people of Israel could only wait and wonder, keeping themselves busy in the fields and distracted in the orchards until the count of the omer grew full.

At long last, no matter their means and wherever their homes, God's dispersed children packed up their carriages, donkeys, or modest carts, filled them with their baskets threaded with gold or silver or straw, and set out for Jerusalem. The burgeoning network of wide Roman roads channeled the flow of these Feast of Weeks pilgrims from across the entire empire, stretching from Europe in the northwest to Arabia in the southeast, toward the geographic and spiritual heart of the nation.

Traversing the countryside with firstfruits in tow, travelers stayed with family and friends along the route. Where towns were few and far between, pilgrims lodged together in large, open-air hostels known as "a place for strangers."[201] Generous Jews living outside the Holy Land typically sponsored these hostels, covering all the lodging costs for their brethren who were traveling to the Temple. These large way stations allowed people to rest safely while also keeping beasts, carriages, and carts protected in center courtyards visible from each of the doorless rooms. What was lost in privacy was gained in community. Children frolicked with one another among the menagerie in the middle, and adults visited with family and friends, old and new. While the accommodations were simple, they were filled with generosity and kindness, leading to the rabbinic saying that "the entertainment of travelers was as great a matter as the reception of the Shechinah."[202] That summer, conversations in homes and way stations were likely filled with musings and theories about the rabbi Jesus and His rumored resurrection.

By the time the swarm of festal pilgrims converged in Jerusalem, the disciples of Jesus were already there and had been for some time. There, at the scarred feet of the resurrected Jesus, they had been learning about the kingdom of God (Acts 1:3). At the same time, of course, they had also been counting the days until the Feast of Weeks, just as they had always done. In the final days leading up to the feast, they hadn't budged from Jerusalem, because Jesus had told them not to. Before ascending into the clouds in front of their astonished eyes, He had instructed them to wait until they would be baptized—not with water, but this time with the Holy Spirit (Acts 1:4–5). Even if the disciples didn't quite understand, they were most certainly done with the days of doubting anything the now-resurrected-and-ascended Jesus told them.

And so the disciples remained in Jerusalem, counting the days until the Feast of Weeks, until Pentecost. They are, in fact, one and the same. "Pentecost" is simply Greek for "fiftieth." So whether counting days (Pentecost) or weeks (Shavuot), God's people have been celebrating this feast every single year since the days in the desert.

Of course, this particular Pentecost would be very different, and the countdown—or count-up—was different, too. On one hand, the disciples counted the days of the omer, and on the other hand, they counted the days since Jesus had left them. With each sunset, they probably wondered how many more days it would be until they would be "clothed with power," whatever that meant (Luke 24:49 NIV). It can be torture to wait when we don't know how long the waiting will last. In hindsight, the disciples would see the answers with unveiled eyes. In the meantime, while they waited, Jesus's followers did all that they knew to do: They continued counting the days toward Pentecost. Without realizing it, though, they were also counting toward the very day for which Jesus had told them to wait.

On the fiftieth day, as dusk began to fall, the nation of rejoicing worshipers made their way toward the Temple courts. The counting was over. It was time to wave loaves and lambs and to offer thanks. In the morning, everyone began presenting their firstfruits to the priests who stood waiting for them in the courts. Shouldering their baskets, offerors walked toward the Temple, ready to finally offer their bounty to God. The crowd was probably growing larger and larger as the traditional text of Exodus 20 was read aloud. There, in the courts, the gathered nation took in Moses's words, visualizing that fiftieth day of thunder and lightning on Mount Sinai. Maybe the people were pondering what it had been like to witness God's visible voice rippling out from Mount Sinai to the ends of the earth. Maybe they were imagining the aroma of heaven that accompanied His voice with each of the "Ten Utterances"—the Ten Commandments.

Then, suddenly, it was happening again. Happening anew. The sound of a violent wind and the commotion of countless voices drew throngs of pilgrims like a magnet to a house where flames from heaven were once again descending on God's people. Again, God's visible voice began inscribing His covenant—a *new* covenant, the *foretold* covenant—on hearts of flesh instead of tablets of stone.

> And afterward, I will pour out my Spirit on all people. Your sons and daughters will prophesy, your old men will dream dreams, your young men will see visions. Even on my servants, both men and women, I will pour out my Spirit in those days.
>
> (Joel 2:28–29 NIV)

> On the day of Pentecost all the believers were meeting together in one place. Suddenly, there was a sound from heaven like the roaring of a mighty windstorm, and it filled the house where they were sitting. Then, what looked like flames or tongues of fire appeared and settled on each of them. And everyone present was filled with the Holy Spirit and began speaking in other languages, as the Holy Spirit gave them this ability.
>
> At that time there were devout Jews from every nation living in Jerusalem. When they heard the loud noise, everyone came running, and they were bewildered to hear their own languages being spoken by the believers.
>
> They were completely amazed. "How can this be?" they exclaimed. "These people are all from Galilee, and yet we hear them speaking in our own native languages!"
>
> (Acts 2:1–8 NLT)

In one glorious moment—on the anniversary of the long-ago day when heaven's wind swept God's fragrant voice throughout the whole earth in every human language—the roar of a mighty windstorm again swept through the people gathered in His name.[203] In Sinai, the Israelites had seen the voice of God, and now here in Jerusalem, in another supernatural blaze, the voice of God became visible once more. Tongues of fire swirled not at a distance atop a mountain, but reached down to settle on individual people. In a moment of mass synesthesia, sounds were seen and their force was felt. The whole thing sounds a bit hallucinogenic. Which is exactly what many in the growing crowd assumed as the group burst outside: "They are full of sweet wine and are drunk!" (Acts 2:13 AMP). But the ridicule couldn't silence the reality that foreign languages were simultaneously spilling out of uneducated mouths. Nor could the mockers silence the multilingual message of the "wonderful things God [had] done" (Acts 2:11 NLT).

The story of Jesus's redemption made its way to the ears of Parthians, Medes, Elamites, and Mesopotamians who had traveled from the east. It made its way to the ears of visitors from Cappadocia, Phrygia, and Pamphylia in the north. The news was understood by pilgrims traveling from the west, including Rome, Crete, and Cyrene and Asia, Libya, and Egypt. Arabians from the southeast heard it clearly, as did all the converts to Judaism hailing from who knows where else.* Of course, the Jews of Israel saw and heard it all, too. A great many of them would likely point to this supernatural spectacle as the tipping point of their faith.

Nearly everyone in that shell-shocked crowd was a Jew who had simply answered God's biblical call to come celebrate the feast in Jerusalem. Now God was calling them each personally, in their own unique languages and dialects, through the lips of unwitting, unschooled translators. The curse of disunity and confusion that had been rippling down from Babel was suddenly reversed in one thunderous moment. Instead of finding themselves divided by language, this multinational assembly found themselves united by a single spoken message: The promised Messiah had arrived and had conquered sin and death, shattering the barriers between people and God and between people and one another (Eph. 2:13–18).

In response to the scoffers' scoffing, Peter—the one previously known for speaking without thinking—now rose to his feet to explain the gospel message. He brilliantly wove together Scriptures, prophecies, and the life of Jesus. The fisherman hadn't lost any of his passion—in fact, it had grown exponentially. But now it was anchored and focused. Humbled by his triple denial, illuminated by Jesus's post-resurrection teaching, and filled with the power of the promised Holy Spirit, Peter was finally ready to step into the calling that God had always planned for him (Matt. 16:18).

*Gentile converts were a significant proportion within the Jewish people in the first century, potentially the majority (Stern, *The Jewish New Testament*, 222).

Peter reminded his fellow Jews of God's promise, spoken through Joel, that one day He would pour out His Spirit on all people—sons and daughters, men and women, weak and strong (Acts 2:17–18; Joel 2:28–29; 3:1–2).[204] He quoted King David's messianic psalms. He recounted Jesus's life, death, and resurrection. Then, concluding his sermon in the midst of the pilgrim throng, Peter proclaimed: "Therefore, let the whole house of Isra'el know beyond doubt that God has made him both Lord and Messiah" (Acts 2:36 CJB).

Even though Peter's audience that day was primarily Jewish, he made it absolutely clear that the good news of mercy, grace, and peace was meant for Jews and gentiles alike, all over the world (Acts 2:21, 39). And an astounding number of people responded to this invitation: Three thousand professed faith in Jesus as Messiah that very day and entered the waters of baptism (Acts 2:41). It was a staggering increase from the cluster of just one hundred and twenty disciples in Jerusalem after Jesus's ascension (Acts 1:15). This multiplication of believers evokes an image of loaves and fishes in the hands of Jesus. Day by day that week, while Israel's pilgrims kept adding baskets of bounty to the sanctuary, the Spirit kept growing the messianic community. In a matter of weeks, the number more than doubled (Acts 4:4). The Messiah's call to share the good news of His grace and redemption was blossoming into abounding fruit (Acts 1:8). A new kind of harvest was burgeoning, even as rejection and persecution increased as well. These were hardships Jesus had warned them would come, but they were hardships that had now lost their sting in the light of His glory and grace.

The community of Jerusalem believers continued to share the good news of Jesus in the shadow of the Temple. The Pentecost pilgrims, meanwhile, carried it outward immediately, launching Jesus's Great Commission simply by going home.

> But you are to be given power when the Holy Spirit has come to you. You will be witnesses to me, not only in Jerusalem, not only throughout Judea, not only in Samaria, but to the very ends of the earth!
>
> (Acts 1:8 PHILLIPS)

These visitors from every nation under heaven simply set off on their journeys back home, winding their way down the Roman roads and branching out in all directions (Acts 2:5). Along the way, they would share with people the meaning of Jesus's Passover crucifixion and resurrection. They would tell their neighbors back home all about the *Ruach HaKodesh*—the Holy Spirit—descending in flames and speaking to them in Latin, Assyrian, Median, and countless other languages. The pilgrims would describe the full, risen loaves waving in the air and the sudden fullness now within them. *Remember the counting we had been praying over every night since Passover? We thought we were counting to the gifts we would bring to God, but all along, we were counting to the gift He would give us!* These new followers of Jesus brimmed over with the living water Jesus had promised all those months ago, during the Feast of Booths. And it would not stop—has not stopped—spilling out onto anyone thirsty for hope throughout Judea, Samaria, and the ends of the earth, no matter the continent, culture, or creed.

Everything changed with that Pentecost. Not only did the Spirit of heaven start taking up residence in anyone who believed in Jesus as Messiah, but the "anyone" really meant *anyone*. Suddenly, the whole world was being grafted into the covenant people, every person given equal access to the God of Israel, the God of all. His mighty arm now stretched out to redeem not only the descendants of Abraham but anyone seeking rescue from the oppression of sin and death. It is what God had promised so many times and had now fulfilled in the most poetically powerful way. Back in the wilderness, fifty days after God's Passover rescue from Egypt, He gave Israel His word and Himself, through fire and voices on Mount Sinai. Now, fifty days after Jesus's Passover rescue from sin and death, God gave all humanity the Word and His Spirit—Himself—through fire and voices on Mount Zion. Redemption is tethered to revelation. From one covenant to the next, our God is the most intentional, masterful, thrilling author of salvation.

The thought of that Holy Spirit Feast of Weeks captivates me thoroughly. Not only the thought of the roaring wind and the Spirit's flames but also of the wellspring of words pouring out of so many people, in so many languages, at the exact same time, with the exact same message. What, I wonder, did it feel like to be one of those unsuspecting translators, with a whole sermon escaping your lips in a language you had never known? What was it like to be rushed by masses of people scrambling toward you, "utterly amazed" upon hearing their native tongue spilling out of your mouth (Acts 2:7 NIV)? God made sure that each and every person was able to hear His message spoken in their own native language. What joy to receive God's words of hope and redemption so personally!

I can relate to that joy—the joy of receiving God's supernatural words of hope and redemption in the middle of a crowd, and hearing them tailored so uniquely to what I could understand. The experience only deepened my lifelong love of words. Even if you're not a logophile like me, there is no denying the weight and power of words, whether they come from lips, pages, or screens. And there is infinite beauty and power in the fact that our God is, Himself, a God of words. In the very beginning, He created with words. Throughout history, He called people with words and calmed them with words. From Sinai, He filled the earth with the fragrant words of covenant. In Bethlehem, He entered the earth as the Word made flesh. And on that one particular Pentecost, God spoke foreign words through human vessels so that everyone could hear with perfect clarity about His covenantal love.

In fact, in a positively lovely and poignant tradition, some Jewish communities celebrate Sinai's covenant by reading a symbolic ketubah, or marriage contract. This fiftieth-day ritual portrays the union between God and the people of Israel. Based on Scripture, and written in the form of a traditional ketubah, the covenantal words are read in the sanctuary just before hearing from the Torah scroll.[205] The declarations are beautiful, adoring God as the Bridegroom, the Ruler of rulers, the Prince of princes, the forever Redeemer. The vows recall His promise to sustain and shelter with everlasting mercy and to give life through the Torah. The only dowry requested by the Bridegroom in this ketubah is a "heart that understands, ears that hearken, and eyes to see."[206] The only pledge He requires is to revere Him and observe His instruction. To validate this marriage contract, the Bridegroom invokes two irrefutable witnesses: heaven and earth. And the ceremony—imagined under the wedding canopy that is Mount Sinai itself—concludes with the most adoring of pronouncements: "May the bridegroom rejoice with the bride, may the bride rejoice with the Husband of her youth, while uttering words of praise."[207]

When I read these biblical vows and expressions of love between God and His people, between God and us, God and *me*, words of praise do well up inside me. And when I lament that I cannot possibly keep all my vows to Him, peace still sweeps over me. Because, in His promised, everlasting mercy, the Bridegroom already knows that I will not always understand, not always hearken, not always see. He knows that I *will* slight Him and forget His words, again and again, even when I don't mean to. Yet the ever-faithful One refuses to walk away from us. His eternal vows cannot end and will not end. And so He, the forever Redeemer of our failings and fractures, clothes us with the Messiah's perfection and revives us through the Spirit's indwelling so that we can rejoice in Him, come what may (Ps. 85:6). It is the covenantal completion of Passover and Pentecost: rescue and relationship interlaced in the most breathtaking of wedding crowns, flowing with the richest of wines. I delight in Him, and—mystifyingly—He delights in me. And in you.

And so we draw near. It's something that not even my ancestors at Mount Sinai were able to do. Because, as spectacular as God's visible voice was, the Israelites still could not come even remotely close to His presence. The weight of God's glory and holiness would have literally overwhelmed them to death (Exod. 19:21). But now, clothed in the perfect covering of the resurrected Messiah and filled to overflowing with the Spirit of heaven, we are invited—beckoned—to be enveloped by the absolute magnificence and love of God.

When I first began to draw nearer to God in those days after Palmyra, nearer than I had ever supposed I could, this word-loving girl was hooked. Because the very first verse of the New Testament I ever read was John 1:1: "In the beginning was the Word, and the Word was with God, and the Word was God" (NIV). In the beginning was the *Word*. In the *beginning* was the Word. The echoes of my bat mitzvah verse—the one I chanted from the scroll, the one I homilized at age thirteen in my synagogue at the edge of a cornfield—rose from the page like the fragrance of God's voice billowing from Mount Sinai on that covenant-making day:

> In the beginning God created the heavens and the earth. The earth was unformed and void, darkness was on the face of the deep, and the Spirit of God hovered over the surface of the water. Then God said, "Let there be light"; and there was light.
>
> (Gen. 1:1–3 CJB)

Thirteen-year-old me could never have dreamed that the same God who created the heavens and the earth with His words would one day pour His words into a tent of human flesh and dwell on earth among us. I could not have imagined that He would one day flood my own ears with His own voice, speaking words of redemption. And thirteen-year-old me—wrapped in the love of family and friends and a suit of purple velvet—could not have fathomed that Elohim's breath—His Holy Spirit—would one day leave His hovering and fill fragile, fallible human beings to overflowing.

I remember reading and rereading the first verse of John, discovering even Genesis 1 being made new in me. The very same Spirit who hovered over the murky chaos at the very beginning, the very same Spirit who pulled the Messiah out of death, now dwelled inside of me (Rom. 8:11). The Trinity—Father, Word, and Spirit—had been living and breathing and moving there in my bat mitzvah passage all along.

Through that indelible Pentecost in Jerusalem, that fiftieth-day celebration unlike any other, the Spirit of heaven made Himself known. Not hovering over our chaos from a distance but personally touching, filling, and illuminating. His tangible presence brought the three pilgrimage feasts full circle, exactly as Jesus had vowed on that last and greatest day in the Temple courts.

And not only for them then, but for us now—for *anyone* who believes. Now those promised rivers of living water, the divine Spirit of God, can flow from our innermost being. Not to ripple around us or to circulate within us but to cascade out of us.

Jerusalem calls us to overflow.

CHAPTER 13

Jerusalem Sending

May the LORD bless you from Zion; may you share the prosperity of Jerusalem all the days of your life.

Psalm 128:5 Tanakh Translation

I didn't understand a single word Ibrahim was saying.[208] Even so, I listened closely. He spoke earnestly in his native Arabic with the Palestinian young adults in the room. Every time he paused, my heart pounded harder. Because, while I may not have understood Ibrahim's words, I knew what he was planning to share with them. At last, I heard him say my name, and then "*Yahud*." At that Arabic word for "Jew," all twentysomething heads turned in unison, their eyes wide and fixed on me.

We had all just spent a week together, ministering to youth and families at a summer camp for Arab Christians in the West Bank. We had shared laughter, music, food, and Jesus. But the gulf between Jews and Palestinians has run deep and wide for so many years now. And so, in the month leading up to that week of camp, Ibrahim and Omar (ministry staff we've known and loved for years) felt we should keep my heritage under wraps. I had been thinking the same thing myself. We all agreed it would be too distracting for the leaders and the campers. The purpose of our time together was to share the love of Jesus, not to workshop a turbulent cultural divide. None of us wanted anything to detract from why we were there.

But now, camp was over. The families had taken the chartered bus back home, and the only people remaining were ministry staff and volunteers, including a handful of Americans. After the week we had experienced together, Ibrahim sensed it was right to tell everyone about my background, right then and there, during our first post-camp leader meeting. He wanted his team to know that this person they had been doing ministry with each day, this person they had been breaking bread with and singing praises alongside, was a Jewish woman who saw herself united with them. Ibrahim wanted us all to experience in a tangible way that our mutual love for Jesus really does outweigh every other loyalty or divide.

So there we were—a roomful of Palestinian Jesus followers, some Arabic Israeli Jesus followers, a few American Jesus followers, and me, the Jewish Jesus follower. If you're American, you might wonder what all the fuss is about. I follow Jesus, so I'm a Christian. We were *all* Christians. What does my background matter? What do any of our backgrounds matter? We all love Jesus, right?

Yes, we all do love Jesus. But in the sliver of terrain that is the Holy Land, no one is ever severed from their heritage. And in that way, the Palestinians in the room probably understood me better than my American Jewish community and my American Christian community. American Jews and Christians, for better or worse, typically see my Jewishness as my background—my *past*—not as my current, enduring identity. But the reality is that, as I follow Jesus, I remain a Jew in my own eyes and in the eyes of my peers in the West

Bank. *Yahud*. In this sense, I am no different from Jesus's first followers.

And so I trembled in the wake of Ibrahim's words. Would these new friends now distrust all the time we had spent together, all the bread we had broken together? Would they block out the memories of me toting children on my hip and braiding beautiful hair and holding little hands on the way to dinner? Would the women choose to forget our shared shrieks of laughter during field games? Would they all dismiss the fellowship of our songs and our prayers? Would they hate me?

No, they would not. They did not. Instead, this group of people born and raised within the confines of Palestine, under the watchful eye of Jewish Israel, rose as one from their chairs and gathered around to lay their hands on me. Every single one of them stepped forward to pray over this Jesus-following Jewish-American girl. Omar led them in Arabic. They prayed for my whole family, those present in that room and those far away. On the outskirts of the circle in that upstairs classroom, my husband, children, and father-in-law bowed their heads, too. The quick picture my husband snapped when we first began to pray is one I will treasure forever.

In real time and flesh, we were living out the reality of Ephesians 2:14: "For he is our peace, who has made us both one, and has broken down the dividing wall of hostility" (RSV). No matter what our different cultures say we should feel about one another, we were choosing the better way. We were leaning in with vulnerable hearts and open minds. The morning after that post-camp leader meeting, our new friends asked me to share my story with them over breakfast, our last meal all together. We talked for a long while, with tears in many of our eyes. Walls were coming down and bridges were being built in that arid, desert camp—bridges that continue to grow and strengthen even now, despite troubled days of war and rumors of war.

The gospel we had shared with other people all week had suddenly been put on powerful display among us. It was the very same gospel—literally the "good news"—that the ancient pilgrims carried down so many Roman roads during that single year of feasts, the last year of Jesus's life on earth. It was the good news of eternal reconciliation between God and people. It was the good news of restoration among individuals and cultures. And it was the good news of God's Spirit now living inside tender hearts of flesh, whether those hearts beat inside a Jew or gentile—or any of the myriad ways people tend to divide ourselves. Because, just as our "body has many parts—limbs, organs, cells . . . [we're] still one body. It's exactly the same with Christ. . . . Each of us is now a part of his resurrection body, refreshed and sustained at one fountain—his Spirit—where we all come to drink" (1 Cor. 12:12–13 MSG). What happened at summer camp in the West Bank between us Palestinians, Americans, and one Jew was the downstream flourishing of that first wave of pilgrims who carried home the good news of living water.

For me, as a girl growing up in synagogue, I had found it curious that God had chosen those three particular feasts—the Feasts of Booths, Passover, and Weeks—as mandatory occasions for pilgrimage. Why didn't He require everyone to come for *all* the feasts? Why didn't He at least call everyone to the Temple for Yom Kippur, the Day of Atonement? It is, after all, the holiest day on the entire Jewish calendar. And if not for that holiest of days, then why require Israel to assemble in Jerusalem for any feasts at all?

In the days, months, and years following Palmyra, as I studied the Gospels with my Jewish eyes, I caught sight of a thread pulling those three feasts tightly together. And I was astounded. God, the all-knowing Master Planner, called my ancestors to Jerusalem knowing that one day, during Jesus's last Feast of Booths on earth, the Messiah would stand up and announce that He was the source of divine living water, the Almighty Himself. God wanted His people to hear it with their own ears and then carry it back home. God called Israel to Jerusalem for Passover every year knowing that one day, during Jesus's last Passover on earth, the Messiah, the Lamb of God, would become the eternal Passover sacrifice and then rob His own grave. God wanted all of Israel to witness redemption and resurrection with their own eyes and then carry their testimony back home. God called all His scattered people to Jerusalem for every Pentecost because one day, on the fiftieth day after Jesus's death, His promised Holy Spirit would bring down flames and loosen tongues. God wanted everyone to experience the power of that moment and then carry it back home. Three times that year Jerusalem had called, and God's people had answered.

Like the two traveling down the road back to Emmaus, every clan and caravan pondered what they had witnessed in Jerusalem. The pilgrims spoke of it all along the sprawling network of Roman roads and local byways. Upon their return home, they began to share this gospel in their own languages within their own communities from Jerusalem to Rome, Judea to Arabia, and to Babylon and beyond. The Jewish Messiah had come not only for Israel but for *all* people. Roman roads may have paved the way for the message to spread, but Jewish pilgrims were the messengers who first carried it.

For so many generations, the multitudes had been joining their voices together along the pilgrimage roads, step after step and psalm after psalm, singing of their spiritual home. The lyrics of each Psalm of Ascent in that pilgrimage hymnal gave them words to express their longing for the peace, stability, and joy found in the city where God dwelled. It was the very same sense of home that had drawn me in during my thirteenth summer. And yet, the home yearned for in those fifteen psalms, in the ancient pilgrimage, and in my own life, was never Jerusalem itself. Jerusalem called, not to the city, nor to the magnificent

Temple, but to the One who dwelled there. God Himself is our home. The anchoring center of our whole selves—the peace, stability, and joy expressed in those psalms—was and is found in the presence of the One who made us.

I believe God called His people home to Jerusalem so that, one day, He could send Jerusalem home with them. The good news of everything that happened there that year could flow down the mountain, just like Zechariah had prophesied. The gifts of eternal shelter, eternal redemption, and eternal covenant rushed downhill in every direction, flooding the nations with firsthand accounts: *The Jewish Messiah has come, and He's come for the whole wide world!*

I wish I had understood this long ago. I wish I had known all along that Christians are, simply, non-Jews who believe in the Jewish Messiah. That they are grafted into Israel, into biblical Judaism. But the timing of the Master Planner is perfect, is it not? One beautiful, sunny Sunday in Virginia, the flood of good news that first cascaded down Jerusalem's mountainside made its way back up the hill, so to speak, to me. And following the Jewish Messiah is, I think, the most Jewish thing I could possibly do.

What now, though? Who exactly *am* I? *What* exactly am I? People ask whether I call myself Jewish or Christian. They are curious about whether I observe the feasts and festivals like I did before Palmyra. You may wonder these things, too. And you may wonder whether you, too, should observe them. What does all the remembering look like today, for me and for you, now that so many promises and remembrances have been fulfilled and made new?

As you can tell from all these pages, I have never stopped loving Judaism or my Jewishness. I love the biblical rituals and beautiful traditions that unite my people around the globe. I love that we all sing the same Hebrew songs with different accents across different time zones. I love that we're all building booths and breaking bread and eating blintzes together in spirit, even though we can't gather in person at the Jerusalem Temple. And so, on this side of Palmyra, I still build those booths on Sukkot, break unleavened bread on Pesach, and eat blintzes on Shavuot—the Feasts of Booths, Passover, and Pentecost. But when I do, I remember both the old covenant and the new.

I hang miniature gourds in my little backyard booth, giving thanks for God's shelter in the wilderness and also for the sheltering blood of my Messiah. I break the bread of affliction to remember my ancestors' suffering and to remember Jesus's brokenness on my behalf. I eat dairy and smell spices in gratitude for God's provision and His covenant and also for the new covenant now written on hearts of flesh. I light candles at Hanukkah to celebrate God's miraculous light. I bake hamantaschen cookies to remember God's rescue through Esther and Mordechai. I blow the shofar on Rosh Hashanah to hail the King of heaven. And I plant trees on *Tu B'shevat* in appreciation of God's creation.

I do these things because I love my heritage and I love Jesus. I observe these rituals because I see the beauty in God's design and because I treasure my childhood memories of the people I hold most dear. And I also celebrate these festivals because I love sharing them with my own little family. I love witnessing their delight and experiencing how it has enriched our faith. I don't change the rituals themselves; I simply bring my current hope in Christ into the celebration. I remember God's faithfulness to my people, and I celebrate His faithfulness to all the world through His promised Redeemer. That is why I call myself a "Jewish follower of Jesus"; it captures the reality that I am still Jewish and that I also worship Jesus, *Yeshua*, as the promised Messiah.

Non-Jewish Jesus followers often express a desire to learn about these things, so that they can better understand our Savior and appreciate His Jewishness. That encourages me to no end.

It's my mission to teach about Jesus in the context of Judaism. I want people to understand Him and the gospel more deeply, and I want us all to grow in our wonder of Him. I wish more people would seek to celebrate the Jewishness of Jesus instead of erasing it. Some modern Jews, even though they don't believe in Jesus as Messiah, do recognize this as one way to diminish anti-Semitism. And so I wholeheartedly encourage Christians to explore the Jewish foundations of their Christian faith in order to know Jesus better and to love Jewish people well.

When doing so, I urge you to take the posture of a student. Make an effort to observe and learn, through the lens not of modern American Christianity but of ancient Israel, and sometimes less-ancient Europe. I encourage you to ask open-ended questions and appreciate what the faith of your Jewish neighbors means to them. I urge you to learn about the history of Jewish persecution, sometimes at the hands of the church, and how it impacts Jews' feelings about Christianity. Perhaps accompany your Jewish friends to their synagogue or sit at their table for Shabbat or attend their child's bar mitzvah. Whatever you do, in all your conversations and interactions, simply remember to put on kindness, humility, and respect, in keeping with the Spirit.

These conversations often lead to the sensitive subject of appropriation. It is a difficult topic. But—as a Jewish Jesus follower who teaches about these feasts and rituals—I am determined to wade into the waters, carrying a deep love for my Jewish people, a deep love for my Christian brothers and sisters, and an even deeper love for Jesus. Interestingly, the question of appropriation is the very reverse of the issue faced by the early church. When the good news of redemption began spreading into gentile communities, the church sought to establish the *least* amount of Jewish practices that non-Jewish Christians had to adopt in order to enter the now-wide-open tent of messianic faith. Their guiding principle was to strip away anything that would hinder the ability of Jewish and gentile believers to fellowship with one another.[209] I think that's a strong guiding principle for us today as well, no matter what the potentially divisive topic may be.

What, then, *is* cultural appropriation, particularly in the context of grafted faith communities? By definition, it is "the act of taking or using things from a culture that is not your own, especially without showing that you understand or respect this culture."[210] Appropriation does not assume malice. Instead, it usually stems from unfamiliarity or misunderstanding. I don't think most people intend to show disrespect or unkindness. And so, the first step to engaging in thoughtful discovery of the Jewish roots of Christian faith is to seek understanding about the "how and why" behind Jewish rituals and objects, and to respect that some of them are too sacred to be adopted by non-Jews. I recommend reading Jewish sources as a starting point, rather than Christian interpretations of them.* And keep asking questions of your Jewish friends, whether they are Jesus followers like me or not.

As far as observing Jewish rituals or using Jewish objects, I offer this general rule: If an act or object is simply an evolved tradition—like casting breadcrumbs into the river to symbolize the casting away of sins before Yom Kippur, the Day of Atonement—it doesn't carry the sacredness or significance of something God commanded in Scripture. That second category includes things like wearing a tallit (Jewish prayer shawl) or tefillin (boxes containing Scripture, wrapped around the forehead and right arm during prayer) or waving the lulav branches. This is when understanding purpose and sacredness really helps. For example, since the 613 knots on the fringes of a tallit represent each of the 613 laws of the Torah, wearing one while

*A good place to start would be *Essential Judaism* by George Robinson. I also suggest reading Jewish commentaries on Scripture to understand the ancient interpretation of passages.

praying is to literally wrap oneself in the Law while talking with God. And because the fringes represent God's word, there is a sacredness to them. We fold the tallit a certain way, pray a certain prayer before donning it, and even bury the fringes when they are damaged. Sacred things are sacred, and misusing them—no matter the intent—can be hurtful to others, as well as to our witness.

Most Jewish people I know would genuinely welcome the opportunity to sit over a meal and engage in conversation about these things. At the end of the day, it all boils down to motivation. I commend anyone seeking to grow in understanding and faith. And if someone desires to better appreciate and respect the faith of Jewish people, fantastic! But since the foundation of Christian witness is to share the beauty, grace, and mercy of our loving Redeemer—just like the pilgrims heading down the highways and byways with that good news—if something optional is hurtful to people or pushes them away from the gospel, please let it go. I think that Paul, the Pharisee-turned-missionary, put it well when addressing this merging of believers and cultures: "Do not think about the things that will help you. Instead, each of you should think about what will help other people" (1 Cor. 10:24 EASY).

That was the goal of the early church as they navigated the expansion of the covenant beyond Israel: helping anyone discover and draw near to the God of all creation through the Messiah. We know from many accounts in the book of Acts that navigating this tension was significant. But those first messianic communities were determined to not block the flow of Jerusalem's good news. Israel's ancient pilgrims discovered that there was so much more to these wondrous feasts than they had ever imagined. With new eyes and Spirit-filled hearts, they understood that, astoundingly, God's eternal shelter, redemption, and covenant were not only dwelling within them but also dwelling just as equally and powerfully in *anyone* who professed faith in the Jewish Messiah. Ultimately, beautifully, Israel's pilgrimage feasts were about walls crumbling down and people being grafted in.

The Feasts of Booths, Passover, and Weeks each had been casting long, breathtaking shadows of the promised Messiah—the one I had heard my grandma speak of with wonder and longing. For generation after generation, my ancestors kept answering Jerusalem's call toward shelter and light, bread and cups, and firstfruits and covenant. Then, in one single year, the shadows ended. There in the city named "the way of shalom," people received words of living water, everlasting atonement, and the indwelling of the Holy Spirit.[211] Everything was made wondrously, profoundly, eternally new. And then God sent the pilgrims back home. "Go and tell," Jesus said. Take all that Jerusalem has given, and go tell everyone, everywhere. Shelter and light are extended to the whole world. Bread and wine were broken and poured out for people near and far. The covenant now extends to the ends of the earth.

I first answered the call of Jerusalem during the summer of my thirteenth birthday. I became a daughter of the covenant, finding myself home in the Land of my ancestors. The summer of my twenty-first birthday, I became a daughter of the new covenant, too, finally finding myself home in the One who had redeemed me on Jerusalem's mountain two thousand years ago. It is a wondrous paradox that, because of what happened there, I am always on pilgrimage and also always at home, because the Gift of Jerusalem lives in me and I in Him.

The same paradox is true for everyone. Jerusalem still calls us all home. But now, she calls us to journey not with feet set toward a city on a hill, but with thoughts and affections and cries and songs toward the person of Christ, the redeeming living water for all of humanity. Jerusalem calls us all to remember temporary shelters and our eternal Shelter. To remember the mighty outstretched arm of the exodus and the two suffering outstretched arms of the cross. To remember the covenant given on the mountain and the covenant flowing from our innermost being. Let us answer that call. Let us all draw, with joy, from this eternal well and be buoyed by its flow. May we never stop carrying the remembrances of Jerusalem back down the mountain, to refresh and revive a parched and weary world.

Jerusalem calls us to go.

Acknowledgments

I am indebted to the team at Baker Publishing Group. Every member of the editing, production, and marketing teams encouraged me by their belief in this work. Chief among them is my editor extraordinaire, Rachel Welcher. Equal parts editor and coach, Rachel grew my confidence in my writing and this project while also stretching me to become a better writer.

Dr. Gary Chapman's encouragement of my teaching ministry over the years has been such a gift. I am indebted to him for his willingness to write the foreword to this work.

It goes without saying that the handful of college friends who welcomed me into their lives, prayed me toward Haden Chapel, and walked alongside me afterwards all hold a profound place in my heart. T.J., Donna, Jenny, Jack, and Travis, I give thanks with every remembrance of you. Trevon, hearing God's voice in your church and then your prayer over me at my baptism are moments that will remain with me always. J.P., your parents' warm and generous invitation to our motley crew is what set it all in motion; I pray that my home is similarly felt as a place of welcome and kindness. And Trish, your awe and worship at the table of the Eucharist has never left me.

Deanne, my steadfast friend, thank you for your encouragement through this project, especially prompting me to think about my story through the lens of my pilgrimages. Thank you to my life group and women's teaching team for praying me through every step of this process. Carol, Rhonda, Emi, and the HRC, you're the best.

I appreciate so much my pastors over the years who have encouraged me to share and to teach and to write—especially Andy Smith, Will Toburen, and Rob Peters, and now David Speakman and Ethan Smith.

I am so very grateful to all my parents, who each encouraged my writing since the day I first grasped a pencil, and for my grandma, who printed my first "book" in her Brooklyn printshop when I was eight years old. All of your encouragement and celebration throughout my life has meant everything to me. This gratefulness also extends to my parents-in-law, who have loved me so well for so long now. To my sisters—Mae, Ilyse, and Valerie—you are the most inspiring women. I love you three so much. And clearly, as these pages attest, I loved beyond measure each of my grandparents, whose lives and faith and love are woven into who I am today.

Lastly, my very deepest gratitude is reserved for my husband and children. David, you had the audacity to tell people I was a writer before I had the courage to do so. Your belief in me has been the catalyst for my belief in myself. Nathan and Olivia, your love of your spiritual heritage has warmed my heart and soul. The three of you are my dearest loves. You are each—and all together—my greatest joy on this earth.

בָּרוּךְ אַתָּה יהוה, אֱלֹהֵינוּ מֶלֶךְ הָעוֹלָם, שֶׁהֶחֱיָינוּ וְקִיְּמָנוּ
וְהִגִּיעָנוּ לַזְּמַן הַזֶּה

Blessed are You, Lord our God, King of the Universe, who has granted us life, sustained us, and enabled us to reach this season.

Endnotes

1. Behrens, *Jewish Congregation*, 6.

2. Wilson, *The Masada Synagogue*, 269.

3. Matassa, *Invention*, 111; Encyclopedia Britannica, "Masada," March 7, 2025, https://www.britannica.com/place/Masada.

4. History.com, *Masada*.

5. History.com, *Masada*; Encyclopedia Britannica, "Masada," March 7, 2025, https://www.britannica.com/place/Masada.

6. Matassa, *Invention*, 147.

7. Matassa, *Invention*, 148.

8. B. Shabbat 99a:3–5.

9. Y. Shekalim 1:1:12; B. Bava Kamma 69a:6.

10. Schwartz, *Tensions Between*, 80n6; Cohen, *Pilgrimages to the Jerusalem Temple*.

11. Edersheim, *The Temple*, 254; Mishkin, *The Pilgrims' Progress*.

12. T. Pesachim 3:14.

13. B. Yoma 21b:1; B. Chagigah 26b:7.

14. Mishkan, *The Pilgrim's Progress*.

15. Crossway, *Psalm 134*; Spurgeon, *Psalm 134*.

16. Peritz, *Woman in the Ancient Hebrew Cult*, 147–48; Meyers, *Women with Hand-Drums*.

17. M. Arachin 2:6; Shurpin, *The Levite Choir*; Rosenberg, *Psalm 120*, 480.

18. Shurpin, *The Levite Choir*.

19. M. Arakhin 2:6.

20. M. Arakhin 2:6; Shurpin, *The Levite Choir*.

21. M. Tamid 3:8.

22. B. Arakhin 10b:11; Emil G. Hirsch, "Cymbals," in *The Jewish Encyclopedia* (Funk & Wagnalls, 1906); Shurpin, *The Levite Choir*.

23. Biblical Training, *Music and Musical Instruments*; Emil G. Hirsch, "Cymbals," in *The Jewish Encyclopedia* (Funk & Wagnalls, 1906).

24. Ariel and Richman, *Carta's Illustrated Encyclopedia*, 40; M. Tamid 5:6.

25. M. Tamid 5:5–6; B. Tamid 33a:5.

26. M. Tamid 5:6.

27. M. Tamid 5:6; Ariel and Richman, *Carta's Illustrated Encyclopedia*, 73.

28. Shurpin, *The Levite Choir*; M. Tamid 7:4; The Temple Institute, *A Day*.

29. M. Sukkah 5:2. The Court of Women was named for its wooden balcony where women gathered during the Feast of Booths.

30. M. Middot 2:5.

31. Rappaport and Gibson, *Nicanor's Gate*, 248. These were the only bronze doors in the Temple complex (Ariel and Richman, *Carta's Illustrated Encyclopedia*, 40).

32. Rosenberg, *Psalm 120*, among many others.

33. Schiffman and VanderKam, *Encyclopedia of the Dead Sea Scrolls*, 715.

34. Rosenberg, *Psalm 120*, among others.

35. Cornfields account for 12.9 million acres (USDA, *Iowa Ag News*) of Iowa's 36 million total acres (World Population Review, *How Big Is Iowa*), or 38.5 percent.

36. *Sukkah* is the singular of *Sukkot*, meaning "booth."

37. Everett Fox, *The Early Prophets: Joshua, Judges, Samuel, and Kings: The Schocken Bible, Volume II* (Schocken, 2014).

38. Black, *Sukkot and the Gentiles*.

39. Plaut, *The Haftarah Commentary*, 689; Bloch, *What Sukkot Meant*.

40. Ackerman, *Shabbat Reflection*; Rabinowitz, *The Sukkah*.

41. Edersheim, *The Temple*, 240.

42. Edersheim, *The Temple*, 240.

43. Edersheim, *The Temple*, 219; Rashi on Genesis 48:7:2 in Rosenbaum and Silbermann, *Pentateuch*. This distance is believed to be based on the combination of Exodus 16:29 and Numbers 35:5.

44. Mishna Sukkah 1.

45. Bloch, *What Sukkot Meant*.

46. M. Sukkah 5:3.

47. M. Sukkah 5:2 (the pitchers held 120 logs each; a *log* is a unit of liquid measurement equal to approximately 0.14 gallons).

48. The Temple Institute, *The Festival of Sukkot*; Eisenberg, *The JPS Guide*, 238.

49. Ross, *Celebrate!*, 214; M. Sukkah 53a:9; Jacobson, *The Jugglers*.

50. During his leadership, Gamaliel established more lenient laws affecting women and non-Jews (Encyclopedia Britannica, "Gamaliel I," September 16, 2024, https://www.britannica.com/biography/Gamaliel-I).

51. T. Sukkah 4:3; Ross, *Celebrate!*, 214.

52. Maimonides, *Introduction to Chapter Ten*, 21; Shitim Institute, *Laws of Lulav*.

53. The Temple Institute, *The Festival of Sukkot*.

54. Edersheim, *The Temple*, 217.

55. Edersheim, *The Temple*, 238.

56. See chapter 4 for additional comments on this.

57. M. Sukkah 3.

58. B. Sukkah 37b:7–10. The waving of the lulav takes place during Psalm 118:1, 25a, 29.

59. B. Sukkah 42a:8.

60. Shindler, *Pocket History*; Pitigliani, *A Rare Look*; Wacks, *The Handbook of Biblical Numismatics*, 53–54, 68.

61. Danby, *The Mishnah*, 178; Temple Institute, *Sukkot*.

62. M. Sukkah 4:1–2.

63. M. Sukkah 4:4–5; Temple Institute, *Sukkot*.

64. The altar would be cleaned each evening during the first night watch (Edersheim, *The Temple*, 220).

65. Herman, *Save Us!*

66. M. Sukkah 4:5.

67. B. Arakhin 10b:16.

68. Jubilees 8:19; Warren, *Paradise Found*, xi, 234; Ezekiel 38:12; Thomas Nelson, *Chronological Study Bible*, 343, 663.

69. Jerusalem Archaeological Sites, *Hezekiah's Tunnel*. The original inscription was carved out of the tunnel wall and taken to Istanbul during Ottoman rule in the nineteenth century, where it remains today. Prior to removal from the tunnel, however, the archaeologists who discovered the engraving made three casts of the writing on the wall.

70. Armstrong Institute, *Hezekiah's Tunnel*.

71. Also translated *Siloah*, *Shiloh*, *Shiloah*, *Silwan*.

72. Yehuda David Eisenstein, "The Feast of Water Drawing," in *The Jewish Encyclopedia* (Funk & Wagnalls, 1906), 476; M. Rosh Hashanah 1:2.

73. Plaut, *Haftarah Commentary*, 419; Bartenura, *Bartnenura on Mishnah Zavim 1:5*.

74. Eisenberg, *The JPS Guide*, 227.

75. M. Sukkah 5:4.

76. M. Sukkah 5:4. The three blasts were a *tekiah* (a single, long blast), a *teruah* (nine or more staccato blasts), and another *tekiah* (M. Sukkah 5:4; PJ Library, *What Do the Sounds*).

77. M. Sukkah 5:4.

78. This was, in fact, a point of contention between the Pharisees and Sadducees, according to ancient sources. The Pharisees wanted to encourage non-priests in Temple rituals as much as possible, while the Sadducees "seemed to have abhorred it" (Kulp, *Mishnah Sukkah Commentary*, introduction to chapter 5).

79. Edersheim, *The Life and Times*, 583; Nehemiah 3:15.

80. Edersheim, *The Life and Times*, 583; M. Sukkah 4:9.

81. Edersheim, *The Life and Times*, 583; B. Yoma 26b:2–3.

82. Some say the vessels were limestone basins that appeared silver because of the blackening of wine (M. Sukkah 4:9).

83. Einstein, *Feast of Water Drawing*, 476; M. Sukkah 4:9; Ross, *Celebrate!*, 213.

84. Edersheim, *The Life and Times*, 584.

85. M. Sukkah 5:1; B. Sukkah 51a:16.

86. Edersheim, *The Life and Times*, 584.

87. Y. Sukkah 5:1:3; Midrash Ruth Rabbah 4:9.

88. Kulp, *Daf Shevui to Sukkah*, 45a:6; Bloch, *The Biblical and Historical Background*, 46–47; The Temple Institute, *The Festival of Sukkot*.

89. The Temple Institute, *The Festival of Sukkot*.

90. Edersheim, *The Life and Times*, 582; M. Sukkah 5:7.

91. Edersheim, *The Life and Times*, 582; M. Sukkah 5:7.

92. M. Sukkah 4:7; The Temple Institute, *The Festival of Sukkot*.

93. Sefaria, *Samaritans*.

94. For examples, see M. Rosh Hashanah 2:2; 2 Kings 17:29–36.

95. Everett Fox, *The Early Prophets: Joshua, Judges, Samuel, and Kings: The Schocken Bible, Volume II* (Schocken, 2014).

96. B. Pesachim 116b:3; Tabory and Stern, *The JPS Commentary on the Haggadah*, xi.

97. Tabory and Stern, *JPS Commentary on the Haggadah*, 6.

98. Edersheim, *The Temple*, 190–91; Tabory and Stern, *JPS Commentary on the Haggadah*, 6.

99. M. Pesachim 10:1–7 (among others).

100. Bokser, *The Origins of the Seder*, 63–65.

101. Apisdorf, *Why Four Cups?*

102. Edersheim, *The Temple*, 168; Strong and McClintock, *Passover*, 737.

103. Edersheim, *The Temple*, 169; The Temple Institute, *Passover*.

104. The Temple Institute, *Passover*; Edersheim, *Sketches of Jewish Social Life*, 27.

105. Gilad, *The Surprising Ancient Origins*.

106. Bloch, *The Biblical and Historical Background*, 125–26.

107. Silber, *Hallel at the Seder*; My Jewish Learning, *What Is Hallel?*

108. Dishon, *The Meaning of the Seder*.

109. B. Rosh Hashanah 11b.

110. Robinson, *Essential Judaism*, 288.

111. Apisdorf, *Elijah the Prophet*.

112. Chester, *Opening the Door for Elijah*.

113. Edersheim, *The Life and Times*, 728; Rosenberg, *The Book of Psalms*, 452.

114. B. Arakhin 13b:1–2.

115. Edersheim, *The Temple*, 168; Strong and McClintock, *Passover*, 737; Mark 11:18b; Luke 19:48.

116. Gilad, *The Surprising Ancient Origins*.

117. Isaacs, *Every Person's Guide to Passover*, 10; B. Pesachim 64a:12–13.

118. B. Pesachim 64a:14.

119. *The Lexham Bible Dictionary*, s.v. "Hosanna."

120. Enkin, *Haseiba*; Edersheim, *The Life and Times*, 808.

121. M. Pesachim 10:5.

122. Kohelet Rabbah 1:9.

123. In the Torah, wine is sometimes called the "blood of grapes"; see Gen. 49:11; Deut. 32:14.

124. Vine, *New Testament Greek Grammar and Dictionary*.

125. The Temple Institute, *Passover*.

126. Nagel, *Israel*, 263–64.

127. Bein Harim Tourism Services, *The Mount of Olives*.

128. Westhead, *Jerusalem's Mount of Olives*; All About Jerusalem, *The Mount of Olives*.

129. M. Berakhot 9:5.

130. Telushkin, *Jewish Literacy*, 548; Moss, *Why So Little About Life After Death?*

131. M. Menachot 8:1–2; Bankier, *Harvesting Before the Omer*; Edersheim, *The Temple*, 204.

132. M. Menachot 10:3.

133. M. Menachot 10:3.

134. M. Menachot 10:3.

135. M. Menachot 10:3; Temple Institute, *The Festival of Shavuot*.

136. M. Menachot 10:4; Edersheim, *The Temple*, 204.

137. M. Menachot 10:4; Shurpin, *What Was the Omer Offering?*; Edersheim, *The Temple*, 205.

138. Edersheim, *The Temple*, 205.

139. Rashi on Leviticus 23:11, in Rosenbaum and Silbermann, *Pentateuch with Rashi's Commentary*; Shurpin, *What Was the Omer Offering?*

140. M. Mechanot 10:4; Edersheim, *The Temple*, 205. This firstfruits offering is often referred to as the Offering of the Sheaf, or the Waving of the Sheaf, but the reality is that by the time it reaches the altar, the offering is technically a dough, mixed as prescribed in Leviticus 2 from the commanded measure of barley.

141. M. Menachot 10:5; Levine, *JPS Commentary: Leviticus*, 158.

142. Mishneh Torah, Sabbath 5:4.

143. Kaufmann Kohler and Emil G. Hirsch, "Crucifixion," in *The Jewish Encyclopedia* (Funk & Wagnalls, 1906), 373; Robison, *Crucifixion*, 52–53.

144. Samuel, *Banning Women from Funerals*.

145. Guzik, *Study Guide for Matthew*.

146. M. Moed Katan 3:5.

147. This is based on variant spellings of Cleopas's name found in the Gospels. Among these scholars are N. T. Wright and James Boice. Jones, "The Unnamed Emmaus Disciple" examines this in greater detail.

148. Midrash Bereshit Rabbah 100:7.

149. My Jewish Learning, *Jewish Resurrection of the Dead;* ben Asher, *Rabbeinu Bahya Bereshit* 2:3:8.

150. Edersheim, *The Life and Times*, 749.

151. Edersheim, *The Life and Times*, 696.

152. *Shavuot* is Hebrew for "weeks."

153. Cherlow, *A Land Flowing*.

154. M. Bikkurim 3:3.

155. Fensham, *An Ancient Tradition*.

156. Sarna, *The JPS Commentary: Exodus*, 16; Harris, *The Land of Milk and Honey*.

157. Fensham, *An Ancient Tradition*.

158. Mishneh Torah, Zeraim Bikkurim 10:4.

159. When Moses asked God what to tell the enslaved Israelites His name was, God answered, "Say to the children of Israel, I AM has sent me to you" (Exod. 3:14).

160. Strassfeld, *The Jewish Holidays*, 72; Eisenberg, *The JPS Guide to Jewish Traditions*, 300.

161. Donlan, *Marion Ruth Schiebel*.

162. Pardes, *The Relevance of Ruth*; Isaacs, *Every Person's Guide to Shavuot*, 26.

163. B. Bava Batra 14b:12; Eskenazi and Frymer-Kensky, *The JPS Bible Commentary*, xvi: *Ruth*; ben Asher, *Shemot* 30:12; Henry, *An Exposition*.

164. Bethlehem literally means "house of bread."

165. Nakhai, *Women in Israelite Religion*.

166. Gill, *Eleven Things About Women*.

167. Knopf, *Converting to Judaism*; Eisenberg, *The JPS Guide to Jewish Traditions*, 299; among numerous others.

168. Eisenberg, *The JPS Guide to Jewish Traditions*, 293.

169. M. Bikkurim 3:1.

170. Sarna, *The JPS Torah Commentary: Exodus*, 145–46; M. Bikkurim 3:8.

171. Emil G. Hirsch, Wilhelm Nowack, and Solomon Schechter, "First Fruits," in *The Jewish Encyclopedia* (Funk & Wagnalls, 1906), 398.

172. M. Bikkurim 3:3:1.

173. Ariel and Richman, *Carta's Illustrated Encyclopedia*, 258.

174. M. Bikkurim 3:2.

175. Edersheim, *The Temple*, 262.

176. Ariel and Richman, *Carta's Illustrated Encyclopedia*, 259.

177. The Temple Institute, *The Festival of Shavuot*.

178. M. Bikkurim 2:4, 3:2–4; Ariel and Richman, *Carta's Illustrated Encyclopedia*, 259.

179. Bogomilsky, *Videbarta Bam*. This number is taken from the thirteen commanded offerings for the Feast of Weeks (Lev. 23:18–19) plus the eleven required for the *musaf* additional sacrifices on feast days (Num. 28).

180. Edersheim, *The Temple.*

181. Edersheim, *The Temple*, 209; M. Menachot 6:5.

182. M. Menachot 6:5; Ariel and Richman, *Carta's Illustrated Encyclopedia*, 265.

183. Ariel and Richman, *Carta's Illustrated Encyclopedia*, 268; Edersheim, *The Temple*, 209.

184. Ariel and Richman, *Carta's Illustrated Encyclopedia*, 268; Edersheim, *The Temple*, 209.

185. M. Menachot 5:6.2; Kulp, *English Explanation of Mishnah*, M. Menachot 5:6.2.

186. Ariel and Richman, *Carta's Illustrated Encyclopedia*, 269; Edersheim, *The Temple*, 210; Maimonides, *Sefer Ha'Avodah: Temidi Umusafin* 8:11.

187. Elan, *Chambers of the Courtyard*; Temple Institute, *The Festival of Shavuot*; Temple Institute, *The Gates of the Court.*

188. Temple Institute, *The Festival of Shavuot.*

189. Edersheim, *The Temple*, 211.

190. Edersheim, *The Temple*, 211; Ariel and Richman, *Carta's Illustrated Encyclopedia*, 269.

191. Edersheim, *The Temple*, 208.

192. Peninei Halakhah, Festivals 13:15:2; Strassfeld, *The Jewish Holidays*, 77; Edersheim, *The Temple*, 211.

193. M. Bikkurim 3:6.

194. Y. Bikkurim 3:4:1.

195. Edersheim, The Temple, 303; Emil G. Hirsch, Wilhelm Nowack, and Solomon Schechter, "First Fruits," in *The Jewish Encyclopedia* (Funk & Wagnalls, 1906), 398.

196. Friedlander, *Pirkei DeRabbi Eliezer*, 12.

197. Shurpin, *7 Classic Reasons.*

198. Ross, *Celebrate!*, 127.

199. Jacobs, *How to Count the Omer.*

200. Edersheim, *The Temple*, 208.

201. Edersheim, *Sketches of Jewish Social Life*, 28.

202. Edersheim, *Sketches of Jewish Social Life*, 27.

203. Midrash Shemot Rabbah 5:9.

204. In Jewish translations, see JPS.

205. Goodman, *The Shavuot Anthology*, 99–101; Strassfeld, *The Jewish Holidays*, 75.

206. Goodman, *The Shavuot Anthology*, 101.

207. Strassfeld, *The Jewish Holidays*, 76.

208. Names have been changed for security and safety purposes.

209. Stern, *The Jewish New Testament Commentary*, 275.

210. *Cambridge Advanced Learner's Dictionary*, s.v. "Cultural Appropriation."

211. Benner, *Definition of Hebrew Names.*

Bible Translation Permissions

Scripture quotations labeled AMP are from the Amplified® Bible, Copyright © 1954, 1958, 1962, 1964, 1965, 1987 by The Lockman Foundation. Used by permission. lockman.org.

Scripture quotations labeled BSB are from the Berean Bible (www.Berean.Bible), Berean Study Bible (BSB) © 2016–2020 by Bible Hub and Berean.Bible. Used by permission. All rights reserved.

Scripture quotations labeled CJB are from the Complete Jewish Bible by David H. Stern. Copyright © 1998. All rights reserved. Used by permission of Messianic Jewish Publishers, 6120 Day Long Lane, Clarksville, MD 21029. www.messianicjewish.net.

Scripture quotations marked CSB are from the Christian Standard Bible®, copyright © 2017 by Holman Bible Publishers. Used by permission. Christian Standard Bible® and CSB® are federally registered trademarks of Holman Bible Publishers.

Scripture quotations labeled EASY are from the EasyEnglish Bible Copyright © MissionAssist 2018, 2024 – UK Charitable Incorporated Organisation 1162807. Used by permission. All rights reserved.

Scripture quotations labeled ESV are from the ESV® Bible (The Holy Bible, English Standard Version®), © 2001 by Crossway, a publishing ministry of Good News Publishers. ESV Text Edition: 2025. The ESV text may not be quoted in any publication made available to the public by a Creative Commons license. The ESV may not be translated in whole or in part into any other language. Used by permission. All rights reserved.

Scripture quotations labeled GW are from *GOD'S WORD*®. © 1995, 2003, 2013, 2014, 2019, 2020 by God's Word to the Nations Mission Society. Used by permission.

Scripture quotations labeled HNV are from the Hebrew Names Version of the World English Bible. Public domain.

Scripture quotations labeled JPS, JPS85, or Tanakh Translation are from the Tanakh, The Holy Scriptures Copyright 1985, The Jewish Publication Society of Philadelphia, PA. All rights reserved.

Scripture quotations labeled LEB are from the *Lexham English Bible*. Copyright 2012 Logos Bible Software. Lexham is a registered trademark of Logos Bible Software.

Scripture quotations labeled LSB are from the (LSB®) Legacy Standard Bible®, Copyright © 2021 by The Lockman Foundation. Used by permission. All rights reserved. Managed in partnership with Three Sixteen Publishing Inc. LSBible.org and 316publishing.com.

Scripture quotations labeled MSG are from *The Message*, copyright © 1993, 2002, 2018 by Eugene H. Peterson. Used by permission of NavPress. All rights reserved. Represented by Tyndale House Publishers.

Scripture quotations labeled NIV are from the Holy Bible, New International Version®, NIV®. Copyright © 1973, 1978, 1984, 2011 by Biblica, Inc.® Used by permission of Zondervan. All rights reserved worldwide. www.zondervan.com. The "NIV" and "New International Version" are trademarks registered in the United States Patent and Trademark Office by Biblica, Inc.®

Scripture quotations labeled NKJV are from the New King James Version®. Copyright © 1982 by Thomas Nelson. Used by permission. All rights reserved.

Scripture quotations labeled NLT are from the *Holy Bible*, New Living Translation, copyright © 1996, 2004, 2015 by Tyndale House Foundation. Used by permission of Tyndale House Publishers, Carol Stream, Illinois 60188. All rights reserved.

Scripture quotations labeled PHILLIPS are from The New Testament in Modern English by J. B. Phillips copyright © 1960, 1972 J. B. Phillips. Administered by The Archbishops' Council of the Church of England. Used by Permission.

Scripture quotations labeled RSV are from the Revised Standard Version of the Bible, copyright © 1946, 1952, and 1971 National Council of the Churches of Christ in the United States of America. Used by permission. All rights reserved worldwide.

Scripture quotations labeled Torah Yesharah are from the Torah Yesharah translation. Copyright © 1964 Torah Yesharah Publication. All rights reserved.

Bibliography

Abarim Publications. "Biblical New Testament Dictionary." Accessed April 21, 2023. https://www.abarim-publications.com/DictionaryG/index.html.

Ackerman, David. "Shabbat Reflection: Sukkot–Beth Am Israel." Beth Am Israel, October 11, 2023. https://bethamisrael.org/shabbat-reflection-sukkot/.

Ackerman, Susan. *Women and the Religion of Ancient Israel.* Yale University Press, 2022.

All About Jerusalem. "The Mount of Olives in Judaism, Christianity & Islam." Accessed March 17, 2025. https://allaboutjerusalem.com/the-mount-of-olives-in-judaism-christianity-islam/.

Altenburger, Nelly. "Why, who and what is Kohelet on Sukkot?" Sefaria, October 1, 2015. https://www.sefaria.org/sheets/17376.

Apisdorf, Shimon. "Elijah the Prophet occupies a fascinating role in Jewish history." Aish.com. Accessed April 15, 2024. https://aish.com/door-for-elijah-and-hallel/.

——. *Why Four Cups?* Aish.com, 1997. https://aish.com/kiddush-first-cup/.

Ariel, Israel, and Chaim Richman. *Carta's Illustrated Encyclopedia of the Holy Temple in Jerusalem.* The Temple Institute, 2005.

Armstrong Institute of Biblical Archaeology. "Hezekiah's Tunnel." June 3, 2018. https://armstronginstitute.org/101-hezekiahs-tunnel.

Aschmann, Rick. "Chronology of the Exodus." Chronology of the Bible, 2022. https://aschmann.net/BibleChronology/The_Exodus.html.

Bankier, Y. "Harvesting before the Omer." Mishnah Yomit 11:13 (2014). https://www.mishnahyomit.com/articles/Menachot/Harvesting%20before%20the%20omer.

Bartenura, Ovadiah. *Bartnenura on Mishnah Zavim*. Translated by Robert Alpert. Sefaria, 2020. https://www.sefaria.org/Bartenura_on_Mishnah_Zavim.1.5?lang=en&with=all&lang2=en.

Behrens, Heather. "Jewish Congregation Has Ames History." *Iowa State Daily*, October 29, 2004. https://iowastatedaily.com/190771/news/jewish-congregation-has-ames-history/.

Bein Harim Tourism Services. "Archeological Sites in Jerusalem: The Mount of Olives Jewish Cemetery." Accessed April 30, 2024. https://www.beinharimtours.com/the-mount-of-olives-jewish-cemetery/.

Bein Harim Tourism Services. "The Mount of Olives Jewish Cemetery." https://www.beinharimtours.com/the-mount-of-olives-jewish-cemetery/.

ben Asher, Bachya. *Torah Commentary: Midrash Rabbeinu Bachya*. Vol. 1. Translated by Eliyahu Munk. KTAV Publishing House, 1998.

ben Asher, Bahya. "Shemot 30." In *Torah Commentary by Rabbeinu Bahya Ben Asher*. Translated by Eliyahu Munk, 1998. Y. Goldman, 1878. Sefaria. https://www.sefaria.org/Rabbeinu_Bahya%2C_Shemot.30.12.5?lang=en.

Benner, Jeff A. "Definition of Hebrew Names: Jerusalem." Ancient Hebrew Research Center, 1999. https://www.ancient-hebrew.org/names/Jerusalem.htm.

Berlin, Adele, and Marc Zvi Brattler. *The Jewish Study Bible*. Oxford University Press, 2004.

Bernstein, Amy. "Women in Biblical Israelite Ritual." Accessed March 6, 2024. https://www.sefaria.org/sheets/361838.1?lang=bi.

Biblical Training. "Music and Musical Instruments." In *Biblical Training*. https://www.biblicaltraining.org/library/music-and-musical-instruments.

Binz, Stephen J. *Jerusalem, the Holy City*. Twenty-Third Publications, 2005.

Black, John M. "Sukkot and the Gentiles." International Christian Embassy Jerusalem, October 25, 2022. https://www.icej.org/blog/sukkot-and-the-gentiles/.

Bloch, Abraham P. "The Biblical and Historical Background of the Jewish Holy Days." Ktav, 1978.

Bloch, René. "What Sukkot Meant to Jews and Gentiles in Greco-Roman Antiquity." TheTorah.com, 2018. https://www.thetorah.com/article/what-sukkot-meant-to-jews-and-gentiles-in-greco-roman-antiquity.

Boaz, Michael. "Christian Seder Haters." *Messiah Magazine*, April 10, 2022. https://ffoz.org/discover/messiah-magazine.

Bogomilsky, Moshe. "Videbarta Bam—Shavuot: Questions and Answers on the Festival Offerings of Shavuot." Chabad, last modified 2005. https://www.chabad.org/library/article_cdo/aid/2836626/jewish/The-Festival-Offerings-of-Shavuot.htm.

Boice, James. "Who Were the Disciples on the Road to Emmaus?" Christianity.com, August 5, 2019. https://www.christianity.com/jesus/death-and-resurrection/resurrection/who-were-the-disciples-on-the-road-to-emmaus.html.

Bokser, Baruch M. *The Origins of the Seder: The Passover Rite and Early Rabbinic Judaism*. University of California Press, 1984. https://greek.rabbinics.org/Bokser.pdf.

Brooks, Phillips. *O Little Town of Bethlehem*. E. P. Dutton & Co., 1868.

Brown, Francis, S. R. Driver, and Charles A. Briggs. *The Brown-Driver-Briggs Hebrew and English Lexicon*. Hendrickson Academic, 1996.

Chabad. "The Story of Samuel in the Bible." Accessed March 5, 2024. https://www.chabad.org/library/article_cdo/aid/134553/jewish/Samuel.htm.

Chabib, Jacob Ibn. *Ein Jacob ("Well of Jacob")*. Translated by Shmuel Glick. Rosenberg Press, 1921.

Charles, Robert Henry. "The Testament of Levi the Third Son of Jacob and Leah." In *The Testaments of the Twelve Patriarchs*. Society for Promoting Christian Knowledge, 1917.

Cherlow, Yuval. "A Land Flowing with Milk and Honey." My Jewish Learning, February 2, 2018. https://www.myjewishlearning.com/article/a-land-flowing-with-milk-honey/.

Chester, David. "Opening the Door for Elijah." Chabad, 2024. https://www.chabad.org/holidays/passover/pesach_cdo/aid/3644595/jewish/Opening-the-Door-for-Elijah.htm.

City of David. "The Siloam Inscription." Accessed October 1, 2024. https://cityofdavid.org.il/en/the-siloam-inscription-eng/.

Cohney, Shelley. "The Jewish Temples: The Second Temple." The Jewish Virtual Library. Accessed February 7, 2024. https://www.jewishvirtual library.org/the-second-temple.

Cohen, Joseph. "Pilgrimages to the Jerusalem Temple." *Le Monde De La Bible* 13 (1980): 29–32. https://www.notredamedesion.org/archived /www.notredamedesion.org/en/dialogue_docsb83b.html.

Cole, Robert Alan. *Exodus: An Introduction and Commentary*. InterVarsity, 1973.

Coopersmith, Dina. "The Book of Ruth: A Crash Course." Aish.com, June 24, 2009. https://aish.com/48972136/.

The Chronological Study Bible: New King James Version. Thomas Nelson, 2008.

Dahlen, Yoni. "For We All Are Jews by Choice." Sefaria, May 28, 2020. https://www.sefaria.org/sheets/240324.

Danby, Herbert. *The Mishnah*. Oxford University Press, 1933.

Davis, Avraham. *The Book of Melachim II (II Kings): From the Metsudah Tanach Series*. Metsudah Publications, 1985. https://www.sefaria.org /Rashi_on_II_Kings.17.35.1?lang=en&with=About&lang2=en.

Dishon, David. "The Meaning of the Seder (Part 3)." My Jewish Learning, April 3, 2015. https://myjewishlearning.com/article/the-meaning-of -the-seder-part-3.

Donlan, John. Comment on "Marion Ruth Schiebel, 89, Was Artist and Professor," June 7, 2016. *The Vineyard Gazette*, January 5, 2006. https:// vineyardgazette.com/obituaries/2006/01/06/marion-ruth-schiebel-89 -was-artist-and-professor.

Edersheim, Alfred. *The Life and Times of Jesus the Messiah*. Hendrickson, 1993.

———. *Sketches of Jewish Social Life in the Days of Christ*. 1876. Reprint, Dream Publishing International, 1994.

———. *The Temple: Its Ministry and Services*. Hendrickson, 1994.

Eisenberg, Ronald L. *The JPS Guide to Jewish Traditions*. The Jewish Publication Society, 2004.

Elan, Yoav. "Chambers of the Courtyard." Tour of the Temple, 2012. https:// torah.org/learning/templetour-class9/.

———. *Musical Magrepha of the Temple*. Beis Hamikdash Topics, October 27, 2014. https://www.beishamikdashtopics.com/2014/10/the-musical -magrepha-of-temple.html.

Enkin, Ari. "Haseiba: Reclining at the Seder." OU Torah. Orthodox Union, April 24, 2020. https://outorah.org/p/66910/.

Eskenazi, Tamara Cohn, and Tikva Frymer-Kensky. *The JPS Bible Commentary: Ruth*. Jewish Publication Society, 2011.

Fensham, F. Charles. "An Ancient Tradition of the Fertility of Palestine." *Palestine Exploration Quarterly* 98, no. 2 (1966): 166–67.

Fox, Everett. *The Early Prophets: Joshua, Judges, Samuel, and Kings: The Schocken Bible, Volume II*. Schocken, 2014.

Freeman, Tzvi. "Do Jews Believe in an Afterlife?" Chabad, 2004. https://www.chabad.org/library/article_cdo/aid/2970/jewish/Do-Jews-Believe-in-an-Afterlife.htm.

———. "What Is the Jewish View on Cremation?" Chabad, 2005. https://www.chabad.org/library/article_cdo/aid/157089/jewish/What-is-the-Jewish-View-on-Cremation.htm.

Friedlander, Gerald, ed. *Pirke de Rabbi Eliezer: (The Chapters of Rabbi Eliezer the Great) According to the Text of the Manuscript Belonging to Abraham Epstein of Vienna*. Kegan Paul, Trench, Trübner, 1916.

Ganzfried, Shlomo. *Kitzur Shulchan Arukh*. Translated by Avrohom Davis. Metsudah Publications, 1966.

Gesenius, Heinrich F. W. *Gesenius's Hebrew and Chaldee Lexicon for the Old Testament Scriptures*. Samuel Bagster and Sons, 1846.

Gigi, Harav Baruch. "On Sukkot Judgment Is Passed with Respect to Rain: The Holiday of Sukkot—Lesson 3." Yeshivat Har Etzion, October 16, 2016. https://etzion.org.il/en/holidays/sukkot/sukkot-judgment-passed-respect-rain.

Gilad, Elon. "The Surprising Ancient Origins of Passover." Ha'aretz, April 7, 2023. https://www.haaretz.com/israel-news/2023-04-07/ty-article/the-surprising-ancient-origins-of-passover/0000017f-e155-d38f-a57f-e757d8510000.

Gill, Cassandra. "Eleven Things About Women in Ancient Israel You Probably Didn't Know." In *Oxford Research Encyclopedia of Religion*. Oxford University Press, 2016. https://blog.oup.com/2016/10/women-ancient-israel/.

"Introduction to Ruth." In *ESV Global Study Bible*. Crossway, 2012. https://www.esv.org/resources/esv-global-study-bible/introduction-to-ruth/.

Gluckin, Tzvi. "What Is the Jewish Bible?" Aish.com, February 26, 2024. https://aish.com/what-is-the-jewish-bible.

Goodman, Philip C. *The Shavuot Anthology*. The Jewish Publication Society, 1992.

Guggenheimer, Heinrich, ed. *The Jerusalem Talmud: Translation and Commentary*. De Gruyter, 2000.

Guzik, David. "Exodus 38." In *Enduring Word Commentary*. Enduring Word, 2018.

——. "Study Guide for Matthew 27." Blue Letter Bible, 2022. https://www.blueletterbible.org/comm/guzik_david/study-guide/matthew/matthew-27.cfm.

"Halakhah: Shulchan Arukh, Orach Chayim." Sefaria. Accessed April 30, 2024. https://www.sefaria.org/Shulchan_Arukh,_Orach_Chayim?tab=contents.

Harris, Mark D. "The Land of Milk and Honey: Agriculture in Ancient Israel." MD Harris Institute, October 21, 2022. https://mdharrismd.com/2013/02/03/the-land-of-milk-and-honey-agriculture-in-ancient-israel/.

Henry, Matthew. "An Exposition, With Practical Observations, of the Book of Ruth." In *Matthew Henry's Commentary on the Whole Bible*, 1708. https://www.blueletterbible.org/Comm/mhc/Rth/Rth_000.cfm.

Henry, Robert Charles. *The Testaments of the Twelve Patriarchs: Translated from the Editor's Greek Text and Edited, with Introduction, Notes, and Indices*. Adam & Charles Black, 1908.

Hermon, Ben. "Save Us! The Meaning of Hoshanah." Rabbi Ben Herman, 2015. https://rabbibenherman.com/2015/09/30/save-us-the-meaning-of-hoshanah/.

"Historic Timeline." Aish.com, 2009. https://aish.com/48960236/.

Isaacs, Ronald H. *Every Person's Guide to Passover*. Jason Aronson, 2000.

——. *Every Person's Guide to Shavuot*. Jason Aronson, 1999.

"The Israel of God—Galatians 6:16." Precept Austin, April 27, 2024. https://www.preceptaustin.org/the_israel_of_god.

Jacobs, Jill. "How to Count the Omer." My Jewish Learning, March 15, 2023. https://www.myjewishlearning.com/article/how-to-count-the-omer/.

Jacobs, Joseph, and Judah David Eisenstein. "Plan of the Second Temple." In *The Jewish Encyclopedia*. Funk & Wagnalls, 1906. https://jewishencyclopedia.com/articles/14307-temple-plan-of-second.

Jacobson, Yosef Y. "The Jugglers." TheYeshiva.net, October 3, 2017. https://www.theyeshiva.net/jewish/item/5377/sukkos-essay-the-jugglers.

Jewish Virtual Library. "Jewish Archaeological Sites: Hezekiah's Tunnel." Accessed October 11, 2023. https://www.jewishvirtuallibrary.org/hezekiah-rsquo-s-tunnel.

——. "Masada." https://www.jewishvirtuallibrary.org/vie-masada.

Jones, Victoria Emily. "The Unnamed Emmaus Disciple: Mary, Wife of Cleopas?" Art & Theology, August 28, 2017. https://artandtheology.org/2017/04/28/the-unnamed-emmaus-disciple-mary-wife-of-cleopas/.

Josephus, Flavius. "Antiquities 3.250–51." In *Jewish Antiquities Books IIV (IV)*. Harvard University Press, 1930. https://lexundria.com/j_aj/0/wst.

——. *War of the Jews: Book 6, Chapter 9*. Translated by William Whiston. https://www.biblestudytools.com/history/flavius-josephus/war-of-the-jews/book-6/chapter-9.html.

Kadosh, Shmuel. "Once a Jew, Always a Jew? Part 3." Kol Torah, 2013. https://www.koltorah.org/halachah/once-a-jew-always-a-jew-part-3-by-shmuel-kadosh.

Kaidanover, Tzvi Hirsch. *Kav HaYashar.* Translated by Avraham Davis. Sefaria, 2007. https://www.sefaria.org/Kav_HaYashar%2C_Author's_Preface.

Kantor, Mattis. "Timeline of Jewish History." *Chabad.* Accessed February 26, 2024. https://www.chabad.org/library/article_cdo/aid/3915966/jewish/Timeline-of-Jewish-History.htm.

Karo, Joseph. *Shulchan Arukh*. Safed, Syrian Arab Republic, 1563. Alhatorah, 2016. https://shulchanarukh.alhatorah.org/.

King, Martin Luther, Jr. "The Ethics of Late Judaism as Evidenced in the Testaments of the Twelve Patriarchs." Crozer Theological Seminary, 1949. https://kinginstitute.stanford.edu/king-papers/documents/ethics-late-judaism-evidenced-testaments-twelve-patriarchs#ftnref6.

Knopf, Michael. "Converting to Judaism Doesn't Have to Be So Hard." Ha'aretz, May 27, 2015. https://www.haaretz.com/jewish/2015-05-27/ty-article/.premium/converting-to-judaism-doesnt-have-to-be-so-hard/0000017f-e9e1-d62c-a1ff-fdfb1f780000.

Kulp, Joshua. *Daf Shevui to Sukkah, The William Davidson Edition*. Sefaria, 2014. https://www.sefaria.org/Daf_Shevui_to_Sukkah?tab=contents.

——. *English Explanation of Mishnah*. Sefaria. https://www.sefaria.org/texts/Mishnah/Modern%20Commentary%20on%20Mishnah/English%20Explanation%20of%20Mishnah.

——. "Mishnah Bikurim (First-fruits)." In *Mishnah Yomit*. Sefaria. https://www.sefaria.org/Mishnah_Bikkurim?tab=contents.

——. *Mishnah Sukkah: Commentary and Translation*. United Synagogue of Conservative Judaism, 2013. https://www.sefaria.org/English_Explanation_of_Mishnah_Sukkah?tab=contents.

Lauterbach, Jacob Zallel. "Passover Sacrifice." In *The Jewish Encyclopedia*. Funk & Wagnalls, 1906.

Levine, Baruch A. *The JPS Torah Commentary: Leviticus*. Jewish Publication Society, 1989.

Ligonier Ministries. "Christ's Tomb Is Sealed." *TableTalk Magazine*, 2008. https://www.ligonier.org/learn/devotionals/christs-tomb-sealed.

Lorenzi, Rossella. "Jesus's Last Supper Menu Revealed in Archaeology Study." Live Science, March 24, 2016. https://www.livescience.com/54154-jesus-last-supper-menu-revealed-in-archaeology-study.html.

Maimonides. "Maimonides Introduction to Chapter Ten of Mishnah Sanhedrin." Maimonides Heritage Center, 1168. https://www.mhcny.org/qt/1005.pdf.

——. *Mishneh Torah, Prayer and the Priestly Blessing 13:8*. Translated by Eliyahu Touger. Moznaim, 2007.

——. "Sefer Ha'Avodah: Temidin Umusafin." In *The Rambam's Mishneh Torah*. Translated by Eliyahu Touger. Moznaim, 1998.

Margit, Maya. "2,000-year-old Pilgrimage Road Preparing for Modern Revival." *The Jerusalem Post*, January 8, 2023. https://www.jpost.com/archaeology/article-726942.

"Masada: Israel, Tower & Fortress." History.com, December 7, 2017. https://www.history.com/topics/ancient-middle-east/masada.

Mason, Steve. *Flavius Josephus: Translation and Commentary*. Volume 1B: *Judean War 2*. Brill, 2008.

Matassa, Lidia D. *Invention of the First-Century Synagogue*. Edited by Jason M. Silverman and J. Murray Watson. Ancient Near East Monographs 22. SBL Press, 2018.

Maymon, Moshe Ben. *Moses Maimonides' Commentary on the Mishnah*. Translated by Fred Rosner. Sepher-Hermon Press, 1981.

McClintock, John, and James Strong. "Passover." In *Cyclopaedia of Biblical, Theological, and Ecclesiastical Literature*. Vol. 7. Harper & Brothers, 1883.

Meyers, Carol. "Women with Hand-Drums, Dancing: Bible." In *The Shalvi/Hyman Encyclopedia of Jewish Women*, June 23, 2021. https://jwa.org/encyclopedia/article/women-with-hand-drums-dancing-bible.

Milgrom, Jacob. *The JPS Tanakh: The New JPS Translation According to the Traditional Hebrew Text*. Jewish Publication Society, 1985.

Miller, Myriam. "The Mount of Olives: Jerusalem Holy Sites." Jerusalem Insiders Guide, 2019. https://www.jerusalem-insiders-guide.com/mt-of-olives.html.

Mishkin, Shulamith. "The Pilgrim's Progress: First Century Pilgrimage." *Segula: The Jewish History Magazine*, 2017. https://segulamag.com/en/articles/the-pilgrims-progress/.

Moss, Aron. "Why So Little About Life After Death in the Bible?" Chabad, 2004. https://www.chabad.org/library/article_cdo/aid/266290/jewish/Life-After-Death-in-the-Bible.htm.

My Jewish Learning. "Jewish Resurrection of the Dead." November 2, 2022. https://www.myjewishlearning.com/article/jewish-resurrection-of-the-dead/.

———. "What Is Hallel?" August 10, 2022. https://www.myjewishlearning.com/article/hallel/.

Nagel's Israel Travel Guide. Nagel Publishers, 1954.

Nakhai, Beth Alpert. "Women in Israelite Religion: The State of Research Is All New Research." *Religions* 10, no. 2 (2019): 122.

Nataf, Francis. *Redeeming Relevance in the Book of Deuteronomy: Explorations in Text and Meaning*. Urim Publications, 2016.

Osborne, James F. "Secondary Mortuary Practice and the Bench Tomb: Structure and Practice in Iron Age Judah." *Journal of Near Eastern Studies* 70, no. 1 (2011): 35–53.

Pardes, Ilana. "The Relevance of Ruth to Shavuot." *Jewish Book Council*, May 19, 2023. https://www.jewishbookcouncil.org/pb-daily/the-relevance-of-ruth-to-shavuot.

Peritz, Ismar J. "Woman in the Ancient Hebrew Cult." *Journal of Biblical Literature* 17 (1898): 111–48. https://biblicalelearning.org/wp-content/uploads/2022/01/Peritz-WomanCult-JBL.pdf.

Pitigliani, Letizia. "A Rare Look at the Jewish Catacombs of Rome—the BAS Library." The BAS Library, May 1, 1980. https://library.biblicalarchaeology.org/article/a-rare-look-at-the-jewish-catacombs-of-rome/.

PJ Library. "What Do the Sounds of the Shofar Mean?" 2020. https://pjlibrary.org/beyond-books/pjblog/september-2020/what-do-the-sounds-of-the-shofar-mean.

"Psalm 134." In *ESV Global Study Bible*. Crossway, 2012. https://www.blueletterbible.org/esv-study-bible/notes/psa/chapter-134?a=612001.

Plaut, W. G. *The Haftarah Commentary*. Union of American Hebrew Congregations Press, 1996.

Prero, Rabbi Yehudah. "The 'Two Breads.'" Torah.org, March 1, 2016. https://torah.org/learning/yomtov-shavuos-v011n023/.

Rabinowitz, Shmuel. "Sukkot: The Sukkah—God's Embrace." *The Jerusalem Post*, September 23, 2021. https://www.jpost.com/judaism/jewish-holidays/sukkot-the-sukkah-gods-embrace-680121.

Rappoport, Jason, ed. *The Sefaria Midrash Rabbah*. Translated by Joshua Schreier, 2022. https://www.sefaria.org/Bereshit_Rabbah?tab=contents.

Rappaport, Uriel, and Shimon Gibson. "Nicanor's Gate." In *Encyclopedia Judaica*. Vol. 15. Thomson Gale, 2007.

Robinson. George. *Essential Judaism: A Complete Guide to Beliefs, Customs, and Rituals*. Pocket Books, 2000.

Robison, J. C. "Crucifixion in the Roman World: the use of nails at the time of Christ." *Studia Antiqua* 2, Vol. 1 (2002): 6.

Rosenbaum, Morris, and Abraham Morris Silbermann. *Pentateuch with Rashi's Commentary*. Shapiro, Valentine & Co., 1934.

A. J. Rosenberg, trans. *The Book of Psalms: A New Translation of the Text with Rashi's Commentary*. Vol. 3. Judaica Press, 1991.

Ross, Lesli Koppelman. *Celebrate!: The Complete Jewish Holidays Handbook*. Jason Aronson, 1994.

Rubenstein, Jeffrey L. "The Origins and Ancient History of Sukkot." In *The History of Sukkot in the Second Temple and Rabbinic Periods*. Brown Judaic Studies, 1959.

Rudman, Rabbi Zave. "Chumash Themes: Understanding Korbanot." Aish.com. Accessed March 16, 2024. https://aish.com/chumash-themes-15-understanding-korbanot/.

Rudolph, Sarah. "Ruth: Follow the Leader?" OU Life. Orthodox Union, May 27, 2018. https://www.ou.org/life/inspiration/ruth-follow-the-leader/.

"Samaritans." Sefaria. https://www.sefaria.org/topics/samaritans.

Samuel, Michael Leo. "Banning Women from Funerals?" Rabbi Michael Leo Samuel, March 12, 2009. https://www.rabbimichaelsamuel.com/banning-women-from-funerals/.

Sarna, Nahum. *The JPS Torah Commentary: Exodus*. The Jewish Publication Society, 1991.

Scheck, Thomas P. *St. Jerome, Commentary on Matthew*: Fathers of the Church Patristic Series. Catholic University of America Press, 2008.

Scheidel, Walter, and Elijah Meeks. "ORBIS: The Stanford Geospatial Network Model of the Roman World." Stanford University, 2013. https://orbis.stanford.edu/.

Schiffman, Lawrence H. "Building the Second Temple." My Jewish Learning, February 1, 2023. https://www.myjewishlearning.com/article/second-temple/.

Schiffman, L. H., and J. C. VanderKam. *Encyclopedia of the Dead Sea Scrolls*. Oxford University Press, 2000.

Schwartz, Joshua. "Tension Between Palestinian Scholars and Babylonian Olim in Amoraic Palestine." *Journal for the Study of Judaism in the Persian, Hellenistic, and Roman Period* 11, no. 1 (1980): 78–94.

Shindler, Colin. "Pocket History: The Secrets of Ancient Coins." *The Jewish Chronicle*, August 29, 2017. https://www.thejc.com/judaism/pocket-history-the-secrets-of-ancient-coins-klvxvm1c.

Shitim Institute. "The Laws of Lulav." https://www.eng.chagim.org.il/STUDY/the-laws-of-lulav.

Shulman, Moshe. "The New Aid for Faith: An Explanation of the Oral Law." Judaism's Answer. https://judaismsanswer.com/Oral%20Law.pdf.

Shurpin, Yehuda. "The Levite Choir and Orchestra: What, Who and How?" Chabad, 2022. https://www.chabad.org/library/article_cdo/aid/5577273/jewish/The-Levite-Choir-and-Orchestra-What-Who-and-How.htm.

———. "7 Classic Reasons for Shavuot Flowers and Greenery." Chabad, 2008. https://www.chabad.org/library/article_cdo/aid/2159/jewish/7-Classic-Reasons-for-Shavuot-Flowers-and-Greenery.htm.

———. "What Was the Omer Offering (Korban Ha'omer)?" Chabad. https://www.chabad.org/library/article_cdo/aid/4354506/jewish/What-Was-the-Omer-Offering-Korban-Haomer.htm.

Silber, Rabbi David. "Hallel at the Seder." My Jewish Learning, April 3, 2015. https://www.myjewishlearning.com/article/hallel-at-the-seder/.

Silberberg, Naftali. "What Is a Song of Ascents?" Chabad. https://www.chabad.org/library/article_cdo/aid/655450/jewish/What-is-a-Song-of-Ascents.htm.

Skolnik, Fred, ed. *Encyclopaedia Judaica*. 2nd ed. Macmillan, 2007.

Spurgeon, Charles Haddon. "Psalm 134." In *The Treasury of David*. Pilgrim Publications, 1885. https://www.romans45.org/spurgeon/treasury/treasury.htm.

Steinsaltz, Adin Even-Israel. "Pesaḥim 120a-b: Eating Before Midnight." Edited by Shalom Berger. The Aleph Society, October 18, 2013. https://steinsaltz.org/daf/pesahim120/.

——. *The Steinsaltz Tanakh*. Koren Publishers, 2019. https://www.sefaria.org/Steinsaltz_on_Jeremiah?tab=contents.

Stern, David. H. *The Jewish New Testament Commentary*. Jewish New Testament Publications, 1992.

Stewart, Don. "What Precautions Were Taken to Keep the Tomb of Jesus Secure?" Blue Letter Bible, April 24, 2007. https://www.blueletterbible.org/faq/don_stewart/don_stewart_247.cfm.

Strassfeld, Michael. *The Jewish Holidays: A Guide and Commentary*. Harper Collins, 1985.

Strong, James. *The New Strong's Exhaustive Concordance of the Bible*. Thomas Nelson, 2003.

Swindoll, Charles R. "Book of Ruth Overview." Insight for Living, 2009. https://insight.org/resources/bible/the-historical-books/ruth.

Tabory, Joseph, and David Stern. *The JPS Commentary on the Haggadah: Historical Introduction, Translation, and Commentary*. Jewish Publication Society, 2008.

Telushkin, Joseph. *Jewish Literacy: The Most Important Things to Know About the Jewish Religion, Its People, and Its History*. William Morrow, 1991.

Temple Institute. "A Day in the Holy Temple–Part 2–Temple Institute." June 25, 2024. https://templeinstitute.org/a-day-in-the-holy-temple-part-2/.

——. "The Chambers of the Court." 2023. https://templeinstitute.org/illustrated-tour-the-chambers-of-the-court/.

——. "The Festival of Shavuot." 2016. https://templeinstitute.org/shavuot/.

——. "The Festival of Sukkot in the Holy Temple." 2020. https://templeinstitute.org/sukkot/.

——. "The Festival of Sukkot in the Holy Temple: The Last Day of the Four Species." 2020. https://templeinstitute.org/sukkot-part-4/.

——. "The Gates of the Court." 2023. https://templeinstitute.org/illustrated-tour-the-gates-of-the-court/.

——. "The Mikdash (Sanctuary)." 2016. https://templeinstitute.org/illustrated-tour-the-mikdash-sanctuary/.

——. "The Omer Offering." 2016. https://templeinstitute.org/omer-offering/.

——. "Passover." 2018. www.templeinstitute.org/passover.

Thayer, J. *Thayer's Greek Lexicon of the New Testament*. Hendrickson Academic, 2023.

Thompson, Frank Charles. *The Thompson Chain-Reference Bible: New International Version*. B. B. Kirkbride Bible, 1983.

Tollen, David. "Aramaic: The Humble Language That Overcame the Persian, Greek, and Roman Empires." Pints of History, September 25, 2011. https://pintsofhistory.com/2011/09/25/aramaic-the-humble-language-that-overcame-the-persian-greek-and-roman-empires/.

Touger, Eliyahu, trans. "Mishneh Torah, Shofar, Sukkah and Lulav." In *Mishneh Torah*. Moznaim Publications, 2007. https://www.sefaria.org/Mishneh_Torah%2C_Shofar%2C_Sukkah_and_Lulav.7?lang=en&with=About&lang2=en.

USDA National Agricultural Statistics Service. "Iowa Ag News—Crop Production." United States Department of Agriculture, National Agricultural Statistics Service. United States Department of Agriculture, January 12, 2023. https://www.nass.usda.gov/Statistics_by_State/Iowa/Publications/Crop_Report/2023/IA-Crop-Production-Annual-01-23.pdf.

Vine, W. E. *W. E. Vine's New Testament Greek Grammar and Dictionary*. Thomas Nelson, 2012.

Volli, Ugo. "Cherubim: (Re)Presenting Transcendence." *Signs and Society* 2, no. S1 (2014): S23–48.

Wacks, Mel. *The Handbook of Biblical Numismatics*. 45th Anniversary Edition. Mel Wacks, 2021.

Warren, W. F. *Paradise Found: The Cradle of the Earth at the North Pole*. Houghton Mifflin, 1885.

Westhead, Rick. "Jerusalem's Mount of Olives Cemetery Running out of Room." *Toronto Star*, December 16, 2012. https://www.thestar.com/news

/world/jerusalem-s-mount-of-olives-cemetery-running-out-of-room/article_a0c1c932-b4bf-53c0-af36-4694380890e6.html.

Wilkinson, Alissa. "Why Christians Keep Appropriating Jewish Ritual Symbols." *Vox*, January 15, 2021. https://www.vox.com/22229063/judaism-christian-evangelical-shofar-jericho-seder.

Wilson, E. Jan. "The Masada Synagogue and Its Relationship to Jewish Worship during the Second Temple Period." *Brigham Young University Studies* 36, no. 3 (1996): 269–76. http://www.jstor.org/stable/43044132.

Wisnefsky, Moshe Yaakov. "The Bread of Divine Service." Chabad. Accessed April 28, 2024. https://www.chabad.org/kabbalah/article_cdo/aid/379522/jewish/The-Bread-of-Divine-Service.htm#comment.

World Population Review. "How Big Is Iowa?" 2024. https://worldpopulationreview.com/states/iowa/how-big.

TAMMY PRIEST is a Jewish follower of Jesus. Deeply connected to her Jewish heritage, she was caught by surprise during her young adulthood by Jesus. Her love for Judaism only deepened as she discovered Jesus in her Scriptures and customs and as she came to recognize Judaism throughout so much of the New Testament. She is passionate about bringing these connections to life for Christians. Tammy earned degrees from the University of Virginia and the University of North Carolina at Chapel Hill and has worked in finance, social work, and local church ministry. Tammy currently resides with her family in North Carolina.

CONNECT WITH TAMMY

WEBSITE: www.beginningwithmoses.com

INSTAGRAM: @beginningwithmoses

FACEBOOK: @beginningwithmoses

SUBSTACK: @tammypriest

APPLE PODCASTS: Challah Day